S-I-S

Breaking the Power of
"SELF-INFLICTED- STRESS"

A Journey out of Stress into
Christ's Peace

Peter S. Bailey

PRESS

S-I-S
Breaking the Power of Self Inflicted Stress
by Peter S. Bailey

Printed in the United States of America

ISBN 1-59781-281-1

www.xulonpress.com

Acknowledgements

"My son, let them [My Words] *not escape from your sight, but keep sound {and} godly Wisdom and discretion, And they will be life to your inner self, and a gracious ornament to your neck (your outer self). Then you will walk in your way securely {and} in confident trust, and you shall not dash your foot {or} stumble—*[in stress]".
Proverbs 3:21-23

This work is dedicated to all who suffer from Self-inflicted Stress—needlessly.

It has been a labor of love. I have drawn heavily from the works of John and Paula Sandford and Joyce Meyers without shame. They are still my mentors and I remain their pupil.

Thanks also go to Cecilia Labrecque, Mary Fritz, Albert and Ann Bourgeois, and Maryanne Yacobucci, who came alongside in prayer and love, when it was much needed; to Bill and Florence Matthews for their support, Jos Boelryk for the first edit, and John Sant for being a friend behind the scenes.

I also want to thank my wife Carol, whose editing with scissors and scalpel, organized the work and strengthened the words that remained. Without her anointed skills and insights, this work would never have been brought to completion.

Table of Contents

Preface

Truth is like silver—its purity is easily adulterated. What remains is an imitation, unfit for general circulation. This was how it was for me. As a freshly minted Christian, I carried certain truths, which I regarded as inviolate, but later had to revise or discard. I understood that "my *conversion*," many years ago, meant that Jesus had changed every part of me; nothing remained of the *old man*. I was a finished product, a permanent fixture in Christ's Kingdom.

But I found this "truth" to be seriously flawed. I was "*converted*," but my *conversion* evidently didn't cover such things as *"being stressed out in worry and panicky feelings."* Conversion was a word that, for me, had lost its meaning; it was a worthless relic, useful only for decision cards; a once mighty belief so perverted that it no longer bore any resemblance to the original.

True conversion changes us into the image of Jesus Christ. Like the refining of silver, sanctification of the soul requires intense furnace heat to purify in order to reflect the brilliant character of Jesus in our soul. We need only to say, *"Yes, Lord!"* and the process begins.

Sadly, the Church has majored on the word *salvation,* but only recently has given attention to this matter of *converting* the soul—its emotions, mind and will.

It was like starting all over again.

Jesus spoke unambiguously about this process of true *conversion.*

"His disciples" listened to His blunt message, thinking they had already cut their cloth for the Kingdom, waiting only to receive their high rewards when they got there. But Jesus told them what they didn't want to hear: They were still at the gate of the Kingdom. He showed them how pride had filled their hearts; they were still unrefined and adulterated. To enter His Kingdom, He said, they would need to become as *little children,* trusting, loving, and forgiving, humbly desiring to change. His meaning was clear: they would need to be *converted* not only in their spirit man, but also in their soul and body.

In his letter to the Thessalonians, the Apostle Paul reveals that we are a tri-part being (1 Thessalonians 5:23). It gradually dawned on me that all three parts need to be converted! All the old nature needs to be consumed in the fire of the Holy Spirit.

1. **The Spirit** within us is first *converted* from its passive, dead state, and quickened toward God. Fellowship with the Godhead is re-established. The Holy Spirit then works to align the other two parts of man to God.

2. **The Soul** is then *converted* in the process of "sanctification," with every negative emotion and thought being converted into positive expressions of Christ. By the work of the Holy Spirit, every vestige of *self* is destroyed. In its place Christ's image is formed in us.

3. **The Body** is God's dwelling place, the temple to contain the soul and spirit. When the body follows the lead of the soul, the vessel becomes carnal; when the body chooses to be controlled by the desires of the Spirit, it becomes a spiritual instrument for Christ's service and future glorification (Romans 8: 5).

True conversion, then, is a radical process that touches and redeems every part of man for God. We need to invite Jesus to renew each part; He will not do it unless we ask Him!

This same powerful Truth was shown to the Disciple Peter. *"But*

I have prayed especially for you [Peter], that your [own] faith may not fail; and when you yourself have turned again, strengthen {and} establish your brethren" (Luke 22:32). Peter thought he had made it into the Kingdom. But Jesus showed him that dangerous pride-filled thoughts lurked in the corners of his heart. If he did not *convert* them into Christ's way of thinking, Satan would sift him as wheat for destruction.

I had been a *Christian* for over two decades, but that didn't mean I was fully converted! It was easy to embrace church life, its programs, successes, and its giftings, yet remain untouched in my personal feelings and thinking. I had never allowed the Holy Ghost's refining fires to skim off the dross from my mind and emotions.

This was where I stood—at the portals of the Kingdom, wobbling with some homespun beliefs, trying to look the part. I thought I was a full-blooded Christian, waiting for the doors of Heaven to swing open for my abundant welcome. But a series of personal crises suddenly stripped away all pretence and deception. I was made vulnerable enough to see the chaos in me. Painstakingly, I began the process of converting my wayward emotions and thought-life by separating out every ungodly element. This process was life transforming, and this time, my *conversion* became real.

I penned this work at first for my own benefit, until I found that its keys and principles helped others walk out of their own stress. I pray that this book will also help you.

Introduction

This book was born out of a therapeutic need! An insatiable hunger to be well and free from the agonizing stresses in my body, emotions, and mind, eventually drove me into the Word of God. I was desperate to understand how *"worry and anxiety"* could rob me of Christ's peace so easily. The answer was there, hidden, waiting to be revealed! This is my journey of discovery in Christ's Word, which walked me out of debilitating stress into the delight, comfort, and peace of Jesus. This journey is also for you!

Self-Inflicted Stress is a sickness we put on ourselves. It is our responsibility to see it, accept it, and put it off! By applying three simple keys and a few principles God revealed to me, I was able not only to manage and ward off attacks in my body, but also to eliminate stress roots in my emotions and mind. The result: peace began to flow in me; Jesus became more real than ever.

I had held off asking questions about the stress build-up in me, hoping that someday its fears would somehow just disappear. But that day never came. No matter how hard I tried to will my rampaging worries and anxieties down, they came back, sometimes even worse. It never occurred to me that my complaint was *stress* and that I could bring it before God for a remedy, that is, until extreme fatigue, spiking blood pressure, and other typical panic attack symptoms sent me time and again to the hospital. *"Hope deferred makes the heart sick, but when the desire is fulfilled, it is a tree of life* (Proverbs 13:12). I was ripe for change.

But did I want to change deep down? Jesus is willing *to "fulfill the desires of those who reverently {and} worshipfully fear Him; He also will hear their cry and will save them"* (Psalms 145:19). Did I have a strong enough desire to accept more change? The more I came to Him asking questions, the more this desire to change, be well and free, became an all-consuming passion.

I knew that doing it God's way would mean a radical change in my lifestyle. If stress was to go, I would need to place myself on the altar each day, *determined* to allow God to surgically expose every fault in His light. I would need to revise the way I thought about myself, about others and even about God. He would need to lead me from my encased blackened *self-life* into His floodlit presence. God is who He says He is; all that was required of me was that I yield to Him.

It didn't mean a rendezvous with my inner self on some mountain top, away from all stress. It meant stirring up the gift that Jesus had already planted within me when I became a Christian. It meant learning how to yield to His love, peace, and joy in the Holy Spirit. I had never done this in my efforts to quell my raging stress.

Now it was God's turn to fight for me. I carried His sword.

I am convinced now that any serious student of the Word of God can walk into freedom from physical, emotional and mental stress. By knowing how stress builds in our bodies, emotions, and minds, we acquire a weapon strong enough to defeat the enemy who tries to bind us in worry and fear.

By diligently applying the keys presented in this book, even the root causes of stress can be eliminated. Peace always follows our willingness and obedience.

Many of the principles and thoughts contained in this book were originally given in churches as sermons, and, in small groups, as seminars. I have set them down in this book as directed by the Holy Spirit.

PART I

Managing the Symptoms of Stress

CHAPTER ONE

A new word in my vocabulary– "Stress!"

"The testimony of the LORD is sure, making wise the simple."
(Psalms 19:7b)

*"The Lord preserves the simple; I was brought low,
and He helped me {and} saved me."*
(Psalms 116:6)

On a grey November day in 2000, I left Brantford General Hospital in the early hours of the morning, pondering an awful truth: *If I didn't change my ways, I would end up a physical and emotional wreck!*

Five visits to the emergency room! Once again the doctor could find nothing wrong! *"It's not your heart,"* he said in a familiar refrain. Hooked up to monitors, I watched as my blood pressure spiked wildly over 200. My face, beet red one minute, would be ashen the next. Weakness left me struggling for breath. Always fear—rolling over me in waves. With each visit I would pronounce the end of my years as a pastor in a mainline denominational church.

The doctor concluded with this: *"It's not physical; it has to be biochemical. Would you like to talk with our arbitrage nurse?* I wasn't sure what an arbitrage nurse was, but I was desperate for answers. *"She's in mental health,"* he added. I swallowed my pride and agreed.

The nurse ushered me to a side room and squared off in front of me: *"You're not going crazy!"* she said, bluntly, as though she knew exactly what I was thinking. *"But the problem is you!"*

Then, pointing her long finger at me she spelled it out: *"What you've been experiencing is STRESS."* Slowly she added: *"It was an ... A-N-X-I-E-T-Y P-A-N-I-C A-T-T-A-C-K!"*

She then proceeded to unfold the workings of this mysterious malady. I sat fascinated as she explained the problem so simply. She told me *"Stress attacks are far more common than is generally known."* She assured me that my condition was not life threatening, and that it could be easily managed. *"The first thing you must realize is that stress starts in the mind,"* she said. *"In other words, it's your fault!"*

I was stunned!

Her explanation seemed unrealistic...too simple! How could she say that all those vicious attacks on my mind and body, especially over the past three years, were all my doing! So many nights I had been jerked awake, sensing some terrible danger—cold sweats lathering my body. How many times had I been sucked into a spiraling whirlpool of dark fears, as though my life was coming to an abrupt end? There had to be a medical remedy, I reasoned. But she was adamant. *"You're not breathing right,"* she observed, *"and your thinking is all wrong!"*

She ordered me to sit up straight in the chair: *"I'm going to teach you how to breathe!"*

"Take a deep breath...fill your entire body cavity with air. Hold for a few seconds, then blow s-l-o-w-l-y out of your pursed mouth, like this."

I watched her and did the same. *"Good,"* she said. *"As you breathe out, think of something pleasant—a lake or field, or some good time you have had. Practice this technique whenever you feel an attack coming on. After one week, you will be in control."*

She rose to leave, adding: *"Stress builds from negative thinking. You're trying to figure out tomorrow!"* With that she was gone.

Suddenly, my strange sickness had a name—"Stress." I took a

quick glance over the past five years. There had been many times when stress symptoms had laid me low for short periods, but I never knew what they were. I had brushed them aside. They never lasted long enough for me to take note of them. But the severity of them had increased in the last 2-3 years, enough to give me serious problems.

I mulled over what she had said on the way home. Was she right? Is the cure that simple? I practiced her technique in the car as the attack waves came over me every few minutes. And it worked!

Over the next few days, I sensed a great excitement within me. God had clearly spoken through this nurse. In His great love for me, He had shown me a huge door and had handed me a bunch of keys. I could accept or reject them. If I were to use the keys, I knew it would open a way I had never traveled before. It would be life changing.

I accepted the challenge. I began to study "Stress" and its effects upon my body, soul and spirit; after several years, I am now able to share with you the specific keys I was given.

If you take this journey with me to the end of this book, and make the necessary lifestyle changes, I feel confident that your stress will come under new management and that by applying the keys you will enjoy a deeper measure of Christ's peace... as they did for me.

THE ORIGIN OF ALL STRESS

I began to search the book of Genesis for help. I had looked at the creation story many times, but had never seen before that the Genesis world could apply to my own condition. Now I saw it!

The Genesis world was in chaos. Darkness and confusion shrouded the frigid planet...a worthless relic hung in space. How did God bring order and life into this ice-bound ball of waste? He simply SEPARATED away the mess! God spoke and the binding elements were loosed from the earth (Genesis 1:2-3). Only then did the foundations of the earth appear at His command. God used a simple process to create His masterpiece—the Process of SEPARATION.

Key #1: Separation starts the process of creating order out of chaos.

The story of Creation graphically illustrated my own tangled, stressed out world! In times of anxiety attacks, I felt empty, worthless, and suspended in the cold, primeval world—of *myself*. In those moments, I had no idea who I was.

How could this fear-filled ball of confusion that was me, have a purpose? Did God even love me? Even though I was a Spirit-filled Christian, and a pastor, I felt separated from God, locked in a world of fear. *"But your iniquities have made a separation between you and your God..."* (Isaiah 59:2). *Self* was in the way. My own jumbled mess kept me out of His peace.

In the Genesis story, the Spirit had brooded over the deep, waiting for God's heavenly instructions to begin the process of separation. My heavenly Father had been waiting twenty years or more for me to say, *"Yes, go ahead and start a deeper work of Separation in my soul."* He needed my willingness and cooperation to loose the chains of darkness wrapping my heart and mind. Only then could the glorious foundations of Christ's character begin to emerge in me.

Before the Fall

Adam and Eve lived their days in the Garden in God's perfect peace. They walked blissfully ignorant of the torments that beset human beings: disappointments, rejection, envy, anger. Not one negative word ever passed their lips. The life of God flowed endlessly through them, like *"waters and righteousness as a mighty {and} ever flowing stream"* (Amos 5:24). Adam was the first of God's children to receive Christ's *righteousness, peace, and joy* (Romans 14:17).

This was God's original purpose for man: to live on earth in the peaceful presence of the Creator, for all eternity. Man would be in close fellowship with God as His children and as His intimate friends.

The Fallen world of chaos

But the Fall changed everything! Satan invaded the minds of Adam and Eve with clever, dark deceptions of God's Truths. He captured their minds and brought them into submission to his will. Instead of love, peace, and joy, fears enveloped Adam and Eve. These new emotions caused them to hide from God under a tree in shame and guilt and confusion. Satan had won a great victory. Mankind had been thrown back into the primal darkness, the chaos, and emptiness of the unredeemed planet.

From that time on, the world, the flesh, and the devil conspire to destroy the hearts and minds of every individual.

It's as though the human race has been lowered *10,000* feet in a bathysphere and subjected to the crushing ocean pressures of sin. Fears of all kinds envelop us, assaulting us unrelentingly in our spirit, soul and body. Every individual struggles to be free. There is a sense of urgency in every heart to be lifted up, out of this fear-filled darkness to return to God. But we cannot: the pressures of the sea are too great. They weigh us down. This is the origin of all stress in mankind.

When I first became a Christian, I had no idea that God had equipped me with an equalizing power, sufficient to more than conquer these forces. I knew that the Holy Spirit dwelt within me. I could confess: *"Greater is He that is in you, than he that is in the world"* (1 John 4:4, KJV), but in reality, the peace I longed for was far off. Fear was my master! I passively accepted these dark pressures as a part of my life. Their worries and anxieties simply flowed through me, unchecked, in endless streams.

I needed someone who could help me separate from every ungodly source that had invaded my soul. I found one—the Lord Jesus Christ. Did He not say that: *"I came into this world for judgment (as a **Separator**, in order that there may be a **separation** between those who believe on Me and those who reject Me), to make the sightless see…"* (John 9:39; Emphasis added)? Ever since I received Christ as my personal Savior, I had had the SEPARATOR (Matthew 2:23) dwelling within me all along and hadn't realized it.

Saint Augustine said that anxiety functions as a call of God to return to Himself: *"You have made us for Yourself and restless is our heart until it rests in You"* (Augustine, Confessions 1:1).

There is a sense of urgency in every heart to be lifted up, out of this fear-filled darkness.

All of mankind is enveloped and shaped in this sea of fear. *"Behold, I was brought forth in (a state of) iniquity; my mother was sinful who conceived me (and I too am sinful)"* (Psalms 51:5). If I were to experience any degree of rest and freedom, then God would have to lift me from this ocean of anxiety into His peace. He would need to show me how this same redemptive process of SEPARA-TION could be worked in me.

"'So, come out from among [unbelievers] and separate (sever) yourselves from them,' says the Lord, 'and touch not [any] unclean thing…'" (2 *Corinthians* 6:17). For me, the *"unbelievers"* and *"unclean things"* were **FEAR, WORRY and ANXIETY** and I touched them every day! But where did they come from? Why couldn't I control them? Only God could show me. I asked the Holy Spirit for help. He would be the one to help me undertake the work of SEPARATION in me.

A few weeks after I became a Christian, I went to Israel with the Kathryn Kuhlman tour group. Beneath my calm exterior, fires of worry and insecurity raged deep within. At that time, I had no knowl-edge of how to apply grace to quench their fire. Unknowingly, I was photographed before the stage in Jerusalem, with my arms reaching heavenward in a desperate plea for divine help. Seven years later, this photograph appeared in the Christian Logos Journal, 1981, with the deep fears and unresolved conflicts faithfully registered in my face.

My pastor saw the photograph and encouragingly pointed out: *"That's a before shot! Now we see the after shot!"* Even though I had gained some ground, I was still shackled by multiple inner fears.

I was called into the ministry full time in 1987, and served as "Pastor" in a Baptist Church in Southern Ontario. Those early years of ministry did nothing to alleviate the writhing inner fears in me. I simply pushed them down.

I had yet to realize how that Christ's peace, imparted at my new birth, was actually there within me. It had been *"within"* me all the time. But how was I to release this equalizing power?

Except for precious moments in a worship service, inner fears seemed always to be fighting for attention. Had Christ's righteous workings gone deep enough, I wondered? I believed Isaiah's promise was for me: *"And the work of righteousness shall be peace; and the effect of righteousness, quietness and assurance for ever. And my people shall dwell in a peaceable habitation"* (Isaiah 32: 17-18, KJV). It all seemed so simple! But why was it so difficult to obtain? I wanted a continuous sense of His peace, not just an occasional feeling.

More questions began to surface. If the image of Christ was in me, where was He? If by His stripes I was healed, why was I sick? If I was made complete in Him at my new birth, why did I feel separated from Him? If I was an overcomer, why was I being subjected to the horrors of panic attacks? Why did I experience rapid swings into pride one moment and into shame the next?

I was filled with the Holy Ghost and had been used on many occasions to bring healing and release to others. But the awful truth surfaced: I was still missing God's best! I felt like a phony, hiding my pain behind a pulpit! The church had not grown in the way I had hoped. I began to see it! I had to change first, not those in my congregation!

Carol and I had already taken John and Paula Sandford's six-month Prayer Counseling course on inner healing and had begun to teach its principles in the church and in home groups. I had received many personal breakthroughs, but still the stress within me continued to build. Fear and anxiety pressures were loading a bomb inside me and it was about ready to explode. I had no idea that the strange symptoms in me were commonly referred to as *"stress."*

After ten years in the pastorate, the symptoms began to accumulate and intensify without my being aware of it. The trips to the Emergency Room had already begun. At the start of my journey I knew nothing about this condition, but it was time get down to business.

I invite you to join me.

ACTION PLAN FOR RECOVERY

I Principles

1. The Fall lowered all of us into an ocean of sin. Powerful stressful forces aim to crush the body, soul, and spirit of every individual. These attacks are master minded by the archenemy of our soul—Satan.

2. These highly negative pressures of the world, the flesh, and the devil combine to build confusion and chaos in our emotions, minds, and bodies. Sickness and death is the result. Only by identifying these stressors and SEPARATING them, are we able to begin the process of their management.

II Questions

1. *"The Genesis world was in chaos. Darkness and confusion shrouded the frigid planet... a worthless relic hanging in space. How did God bring order and life into this ice-bound ball of waste? He simply SEPARATED away the mess! God spoke and the binding elements were loosed from the earth* (Genesis 1). *Only then did the foundations of the earth appear at His command."*

Do you relate to this statement in Chapter One? In a crisis, can you identify with the feelings of chaos, hopelessness, and confusion? Take a moment and write down those dark feelings. If you have done this, I want to congratulate you! You have begun to do what God did in Genesis One. You have begun to SEPARATE out the stressors in your life in order to bring forth the foundations of Jesus in you.

2. *"'Come out from among (unbelievers), and separate (sever) yourselves from them,' says the Lord, 'and touch not any unclean thing'"* (2 Corinthians 6: 17).

Do you agree that fear, worry, and anxiety are like the "*unclean things*" mentioned in this verse? Do they "*touch*" you every day? Do you see the necessity of SEPARATING yourself from them in order to walk in Christ's freedom? Why not discuss this concept with someone close to you?

III Prayer

Father, I thank You for showing me the way into Your peace. For years I have been plagued with unanswered questions, and by worry, anxiety, and fear. The result is that stress has affected every part of my life. I have been bound for so long. At times, I am overwhelmed with stress and I want to be free! Please forgive me for being independent, trying to solve this on my own, instead of coming to You. I never realized that I could be delivered from my stress. I am now ready to embark on this journey of SEPARATION and healing. I thank You, Lord Jesus, that You will lead me every step of the way. Amen.

CHAPTER TWO

Recognizing your stress symptoms

"Ah, sinful nation, a people loaded with iniquity…They have forsaken the Lord, they have despised {and} shown contempt {and} provoked the Holy One of Israel to anger, they have become utterly estranged (alienated)….The whole head is sick, and the whole heart is faint (feeble, sick, and nauseated). From the sole of the foot even to the head there is no soundness {or} health."
(Isaiah 1:4-6).

As I pondered this verse, I realized that anxieties were *iniquities* and that my *iniquities* had separated me from God. My whole body, head, and heart were sick. But how was I to find the kind of wellness the Lord desired for me?

One doctor gave me a clue. During a stress test, he asked me to identify the smallest changes registering in my body. Minute differences in pressure and temperature, possible tingling in my fingers or pain in my limbs—were all indicators of my cardio-vascular condition. But looking for telltale signs in my body was for me an unfamiliar exercise! I was being asked to identify and SEPARATE out these minor physical symptoms, before I had any experience of them being there!

In the same way, I had to become familiar with every symptom of stress in my emotions, and mind, even those hidden from me. I soon grasped that stress was manifesting often in bizarre, secret ways. Isolating them took time, but it was nonetheless rewarding. No matter where I was, driving in traffic, standing in a line-up—an inner fear prodded within. It demanded attention and seemed to pinpoint some imaginary danger. It lurked at the gate of my mind, gnawing like a fretful animal trying to attack, urging me to run. This vague pressure under my chest kept me in a constant state of high alarm. Sometimes my stomach would churn; pain would rack my eyes, head, and lower back. At other times, I felt like I was about to topple over!

I began to see that any change, no matter how small—even one thought on the next day's workload—would bring on these uncomfortable sensations.

> **I began to see that any change, no matter how small—even one thought on the next day's workload—would bring on these uncomfortable sensations.**

I was in and out of this annoying state many times, even in one day, sometimes without ever knowing it. It needed a surgeon's knife to find them, and to see them in detail. I fought back with willpower and would gain a measure of peace, but, in minutes, the symptoms would be back in full force. Even after exercise, good entertainment, or simply taking a walk, the sense of *something awful ahead* returned. There seemed no escape from this inner dread! I felt backed into a corner.

After the confrontation with my nurse tutor, I began to connect the dots and realized that all these strange symptoms I was experiencing had something to do with *stress*.

I began to ask myself some tough questions:

1. Did I have a personality susceptible to stress?
2. How was stress manifesting in me?
3. Was I passive, unwilling to make changes in my life?

4. Were my habits controlling me?
5. Were my sleep patterns adding to my stress?

I was astonished at what I found! I ask you the same five questions now in the hope they will help you define your greatest areas of stress:

Question #1 WHAT KIND OF PERSONALITY TYPE ARE YOU?

Did I possess a "personality" that generated subtle, hidden stresses? I found a simple test that gave me the answer. Getting to know my *personality type* was pure revelation. It gave me a fresh perspective. It provided a platform I could use to climb to the next level of my understanding.

In 1974, Meyer Friedman and Ray Roseman in *Type A Behavior & Your Heart,* New York, proposed a classification for how individuals respond to life. They separated out two types of personalities—A and B. We are predominantly one or the other. To my astonishment I found that I had been operating in one type but not the one I was born with! Although this division is simplistic in its concept, it was useful in getting me to know who I was.

Take a few minutes to look at your own overall personality profile:

Type A personalities are aggressive. They opt for the hurried fast lanes of life. There is an urgent need to get things done and be aggressive in doing it! They are irritated by delays; slower people frustrate them. They like to control everyone and everything. Their thresholds of tolerance for failure in themselves and others tend to be low. Adrenaline levels are high in these people, making them very susceptible to stroke and heart conditions.

Type A was my adopted personality type. I had subconsciously cultivated this Type working in Type A environments in brokerage research boutiques in Montreal and Toronto. The pressure to perform and maintain high standards was always there. Every facet of life was time driven. Expectancies were high. This was a period when I pushed to the limits, with late hours and little sleep. Work was all-consuming. As an unwary victim of the worldly clamor for money and success, I sowed seeds that eventually bore fruit years later—in burn out.

I carried this Type A into my pastorate years, only to reap a heavy cost without my knowing it! Being Type A was a badge to proclaim I could get things done quickly and with ease.

Type B was my natural personality. This type prefers the slower, inside lanes of life, going with the flow and with no urgency to get there. But they can be just as successful as Type A. They are able to compartmentalize their work at the office or factory from their home life; and they are more at peace with themselves. Many Type B's work on their own, even isolating themselves from others, as I did, preferring the shadows of life.

With this simple division, I saw the disastrous consequences of being a *driven* Type A and wanted out! I felt robbed and deceived by its alluring bait. I asked the Lord for His forgiveness. Striving is not something God will allow in His Kingdom.

God also showed me that being a "Type B" personality had its own downside. This tendency to work in isolation was a deterrent to Him. It was too easy to hide when things went wrong. He wanted me in a team, as a full-fledged member of the Bride of Christ.

I realized that both personality types were a reflection of *self*. All through those early ministry years, I had worked largely out of flesh—thinking that I was spiritually mature!

Now the Lord had brought me into a massive head-on collision with myself. He was asking me to exchange my personality for His. John the Baptist expressed this idea, when he said: *"He must increase, but I must decrease (He must grow more prominent; I must grow less so)"* (John 3:30).

We all need a Type "C" personality

I saw a third personality more desirable than the last two. As believers we all need to develop a Christ-centered **"Type C"** personality, which is, by far, the most attractive type.

Type C possesses strong character traits, the most important of which is that they draw others into the comfort and peace of Jesus. Their ability to stay calm under pressure is remarkable.

Many times Jesus on earth demonstrated these qualities for us. In the fury of a Lake Galilee storm, He slept in the prow of the boat. The fear-filled, panicky disciples saw Jesus asleep and were drawn to Him for help, peace, and comfort. Jesus might have said: "I slept: why didn't you? Did I not promise you, we would reach the other side?" (Luke 8:22-25).

Many of the best-loved characters in the Bible began their walk with Jesus as Type A personalities: Martha, Paul, and Peter. As they drew closer to Jesus, they to put off their own traits of *self* to display Jesus' "C" personality in peace, love, joy, humility, wisdom, and calmness. Each chose to put on Christ's personality each day. They became Type-C!

Every Christian should aspire to posses the 'Type C' personality of Jesus.

We are in awe at the way Paul and Silas responded to their stress environment in prison. Hours before their scheduled execution time, they sang! Every stress factor working to bring them into fear and paralysis had been annihilated by the Holy Spirit working in them. Even Paul's jailer was impressed! He and his entire family followed Paul into salvation.

Every Christian should aspire to possess the 'Type C' personality of Jesus Christ. *"Put on the Lord Jesus Christ, and make no provision for the flesh, to fulfill its lusts"* (Romans 13:14 NKJV). *"Therefore let* us *pursue the things which make for peace and the things* by *which one may edify another"* (Romans14: 19, NKJV). The degree we *put on* this resurrected personality of Christ, will be the measure we live stress free in a stressed-out world.

When we see the benefits of resting in Christ's peace, it prompts us to stop striving and fighting. Our focus shifts from self onto

Christ. This is what I wanted!

We all can learn this new way, as did the Apostle Paul, by a conscious act of our wills. "*...I have learned how to be content (satisfied to the point where I am not disturbed or disquieted) in whatever state I am. I know how to be abased...I know how to enjoy plenty... I have learned ...the secret*" (Philippians 4:11-12). Paul's secret was grounded in unselfish love and trust in Jesus Christ. If Paul could learn the secret, so could I!

Question #2 HOW DOES STRESS MANIFEST IN YOU?

I felt the need to develop a profile of my stressed-out condition in order to see all my symptoms in an objective light. It was a humiliating task. Nevertheless, it gave me a deeper level of understanding of this complex term we call "stress."

Take a few moments to work out a stress-profile for yourself. Be honest. Your profile will give you hope that stress can be managed. Circle the symptoms that belong to you, and then write them down in the profile below. Step back, and take a good look at them, then hold them before the Lord in repentance.

S.I.S. PROFILING

Physical Symptoms	Emotional & Mental Symptoms	Behavioral Symptoms
Cold sweats	Fearful	Defensive
Flushed face	Irritable	Tendency to blame others
Pulse racing	Weepy	Indecisive
High Blood Pressure	Angry-suddenly	Make poor judgements
Pressures in head	Guilty feelings	Quarrelsome
Chest, neck	Critical	Demanding
Restlessness	Negativity	Fidgety, edgy
Worthlessness	Co-dependant	Lump in throat
Exhausted	Withdraw from	Stomach problems
Restless, edgy	others	Unable to look another in
Tight jaw	Frustration	the eye
Poor sleep, snoring	Racing mind	Motor mouth that won't
Constipation, gas	Depression	quit
Diarrhea	Death thoughts	Gossip, tale bearing, good
Nausea	Suicidal thoughts	or bad
Heaviness in chest	Helpless feelings	Overly dramatic gestures
Tingling, crawling	Denial	and speech
skin		Compulsive, rash
Colds, sore throats		

YOUR STRESS PROFILE GOES HERE

Physical Symptoms	Emotional & Mental Symptoms	Behavioral Symptoms
_____	_____	_____
_____	_____	_____
_____	_____	_____
_____	_____	_____

Figure 1. Profiling your Self-Inflicted Stress

Working through this list gave me quite a jolt. *Self-inflicted Stress* was more than just a physical thing. It had affected my emotions, my mind, and had even spilled over onto everyone around me.

I saw there was no quick fix. It would take work, patience, prayer and trust. Was I willing? *"The Lord is close to those who are of a broken heart and saves such as are crushed with sorrow for sin and are humbly and thoroughly penitent"* (Psalms 34:18).

Question # 3 DO YOU WANT TO BE MADE WHOLE?

I had been sensing this question coming to me for sometime. Of course, I would answer "Yes," but the question, I realized, was a loaded one. There is a big difference between *"being well physically"* and being made *"whole"* physically, emotionally, mentally and spiritually.

Jesus asked this question of the man lying near the Bethesda pool. He lay helpless and had been a long time in that condition. Jesus' question wasn't frivolous: *"Are you really in earnest about getting well?"* (John 5:6). It was a probe to test the condition of the man's will. Jesus set before him a challenge.

Did he want to be healed in every part of his tri-part being— spirit and soul as well as in his body? (1 Thessalonians 5:23; 3 John 2). Was he willing? Had his life patterns become so familiar to him, that he feared change of any kind? Was he looking for attention or sympathy? Did he enjoy being dependent on others? Had his will become so passive he would resist even the offer of being made whole emotionally and mentally? The answer to all these questions came when Jesus told the man to rise up and walk. The man's spirit came alive. Years of passivity rolled away. He was now free to respond to Jesus.

I too stood at a crossroads. Did I want to go on? I had already spent 10 years preaching, teaching and talking about the dangers of living in *self*. But did I want to peer into myself again to look at the mess of my emotions and thinking—especially to see if I was passive toward God in any way?

Was I willing to search for the reasons behind my stress? Or would I settle for a "safe" quick fix prescription for my health problems? Faith spells R-I-S-K: was I willing to risk moving out of myself to probe deeper?

Passivity is a sin

When my wife told me I looked stressed, I would jump in horror: *"I'm not stressed out—just tired! And if I am, there is nothing that can be done!"* How many times had I said this? In reality, a passive will towards Christ boxes our thinking and stops any possibility of change.

Jesse Penn Lewis in the *"War on the Saints,"(Pennsylvania:* The Christian Literature Crusade, 1977, page 51) made this statement: *"The chief condition for the working of evil spirits in a human being apart from sin is passivity."* *Passivity* makes decision-making difficult, even a painful process. A passive *will* saps our energy, rendering us ineffective.

Off-hand remarks like: *"I don't care", "I can't decide", "It doesn't matter",* are uttered from a will that has shut down. Such a person not only feels separated from God, but also alienated from others. In times of high stress, I didn't even know who I was! I couldn't know. My will toward God was passive.

The Church is filled with those who desire nothing more from Christ, other than to know they are saved. There is no *will* to change. Yet, change or renewal is basic to the Christian life. From the moment we receive Christ's gift of Life within us, the change process begins. The Holy Spirit goes to work to form Christ's image in us. But we have the right to resist Him.

When we ignore His promptings in us, it means our *will* has been rendered passive. We set God aside. We have inflicted ourselves unnecessarily with pain and stress. The devil makes our *self-life* so safe. How does he do it? He dulls our will, convincing us there is no need to dust our conscience with living words of faith; so it lies dormant, seared with a hot iron (1 Timothy 4:2 KJV). In this way, he paralyses us from going on with God.

I was right there among them! Yet, I thought I was doing all the right things. Take a look at this simple test to see how strong you are in your will.

SYMPTOMS OF A DULLED WILL

		YES	NO
1.	Do you see change as a threat?	☐	☐
2.	Do you resist change?	☐	☐
3.	Are you un-adventurous?	☐	☐
4.	Do you feel unfulfilled?	☐	☐
5.	Do you lack spontaneity?	☐	☐
6.	Do you prefer not to take risks?	☐	☐
7.	Do you feel your potential is buried?	☐	☐
8.	Do you avoid another's hurts or sickness?	☐	☐
9.	Are you unable to rise to any level of excitement?	☐	☐
10.	Is it difficult to make even small decisions?	☐	☐

Total

Figure 2. Determining the strength of your will

If you checked even three boxes in the Yes column, it means your *will* is inactive or has fallen asleep. It is time to awaken! A weakened will is one major cause of stress. Jesus was asking me that same question: Do you want to be made whole badly enough that you are willing to make a total change in your life? Are you willing to pay the price?

Dana gave up her will to decide as a child. *"I vowed never to ask questions in front of my parents, because it inevitably led to humiliating put-downs. I allowed myself to drift through life; I had even decided not to think anymore. I would let others decide everything for me. It was safer that way! I felt like a pawn, being moved on the board of life. Creativity and initiative had been sucked out of me. My will was controlled by others. No one listened to me anyway. Even when I married, I couldn't make any simple decisions; I left all decision-making to my husband."*

Only when she recognized the passive nature of her will, did strength come into her life. She repented before God for her

38

refusal to make decisions. Within a short time, her decision making ability became easier. Her personal life steadily improved.

In one Church, I asked for a show of hands on this question: *"Do you want to go on with God?"* All hands rose. But when I followed with the next question, the response was far different: *"Do you ever ask the Holy Spirit how you can change to be like Him?"* None raised their hands. With a numbed-out will *self* rules.

So are you willing to destroy every part of your *Self-life* for Christ? *"If you are willing and obedient, you shall eat the good of the land; but if you refuse and rebel, you will be devoured by the sword. For the mouth of the Lord has spoken it"* (Isaiah 1:19-20). God co-operates with us in our decision-making only when we let Him! He doesn't decide for us. He wants our will intact, with freedom for us to choose in every situation. But His love for us remains the same, no matter what we decide. Righteousness is simply activating our will to agree with God and His Word. We *"do the right thing"* to honor Him.

How do we break the power of passivity over us? Begin by ASKING QUESTIONS!

How do we break the power of passivity over us? Begin by ASKING QUESTIONS!

Those who ask questions of the Holy Spirit receive answers. They draw closer to God. The Disciple Peter asked questions— many of them. He was one of the three in Jesus' inner circle of friends. Passivity breaks when we speak out the Truths of God's Word and act upon them—choosing to do right before God.

I was beginning to see my need to turn my *will* completely over to the Lord. Passive people prefer the status quo, not the dynamics of changing into Christ's image. I decided to go on with God. There was no turning back; this was the Way— I had to walk in it!

Question # 4 DO YOUR HABITS ANNOY YOU AND OTHERS?

If your answer is *"Yes,"* then it is a telltale sign you are under stress. *Self* still rules in your life. Accumulating small, secret energy-wasting habits runs like a plague in our society, and afflicts both A and B types.

I was totally unaware of the little things that built up stress; yet they signaled all was not well within me. As the challenges of pastoral life mounted, so did the tensions. I became irritated by the smallest detail. Energy drained from me: tapping keys, pencils, any object that would fit the idea of a drum. Foot tapping, pacing, knee swinging were an obvious drain on me and a nuisance to others.

Stress releases energy in visible habits, but the flesh enjoys them, which makes us reluctant to be free of them. Some we believe help us focus and to think! They help pass the time. Some may even make us feel important!

Here is a list of unnecessary minor habits we found in our counseling, all of which indicate hidden turmoil. Circle those appropriate for you; these are all common habitual, telltale signs of deep inner stress:

- Finger tapping
- Nail biting
- Clacking-grinding teeth
- Nose picking
- Interrupting others
- Pacing
- Foot swaying
- Finger picking
- Licking lips
- Sucking teeth
- Cracking fingers
- Biting lips
- Knee vibrating
- Eye brow pulling
- Hair pulling

- Compulsive nibbling/shopping
- Blinking unnaturally
- Jangling keys

There are many others. No doubt, you could add to the above. You might think foot or pencil tapping is relaxing, but the truth is that with each tap, minute currents of energy are sent to the heart, which says: *"Hey, you are stressing me out!"*

Such habits are often rooted in deep fears of failure, frustration, guilt, rejection, and even the demonic! If the habit is not dealt with, the cumulative drain of energy upsets the balance of the autonomic, nervous and immune systems in the body.

Now that I was aware of my visible habits, how could they be stopped? They were so much a part of me. Once again the Lord, in His mercy, showed me that it was not about me and what I could or couldn't do. It was about Him, and what He would do for me! His Word came alive:

"But He gives us more and more grace (power of the Holy Spirit, to meet this evil tendency and all others fully). That is why He says, God sets Himself against the proud and haughty, but gives grace (continually) to the lowly (those who are humble enough to receive it). So be subject to God. Resist the devil (stand firm against him) and he will flee from you" (James 4:6-7).

Humbly I sought God for answers. These tiny habits were stressors and needed to go. I began to look upon them as God saw them—sin. I made up my mind to loathe them, just as He does. They are not a part of His Kingdom. As I confessed them before God their power gradually lessened and I was able to control them, rather than them controlling me. Hope was building in me.

The Holy Spirit then prompted me to look at my sleep patterns, which had become unbalanced and a source of much stress.

Question # 5 DO YOU KNOW HOW YOU SLEEP?

"When you lie down, you shall not be afraid; yes, you shall lie down, and your sleep shall be sweet" (Proverbs 3.24). God's gift of sleep is for all His children, even in crises! He gives His beloved good sound sleep for every occasion.

As the stress in me progressed, sound sleep became a goal and was something I rarely attained. I thought my interrupted sleep was a by-product of advancing years, when sleep is said to be needed less and tends to be light. Wrong! Sleep, is as important as good nutrition, good air and clean water. Most of us need seven or eight hours sleep a night, to help regulate the various systems of the body. Sleep is part of the body's healing process. It recharges the mind and emotional batteries and regulates the immune system, blood pressure, and weight.

Some may see themselves as *night people,* doing their best work in the small hours. Others may boast of their ability to work consecutive days and nights without sleep, before crashing, but the cost is always the same—internal stress and health problems. Sleep disturbances are important warnings of developing stress.

Types of sleep

Shallow sleep is called **NREM** sleep, while the deeper sleep is called **REM** sleep. We need both types during the night.

NREM sleep or Non Rapid Eye Movement sleeps alternates with periods of REM sleep. When a person falls asleep, they remain in NREM phase for about an hour before entering the first cycle REM.

REM sleep or Rapid Eye Movement Sleep is the deepest sleep of the night. This is when most of the dreaming takes place, with many dreams being vivid and easy to recall. About a quarter of the night sleep is in this REM phase. REM sleep is needed to refresh the memory bank, information sorting and learning centers of the brain. Little wonder, my short-term memory felt like it was going. My ability to process information lacked the freshness I needed.

Broken Sleep –A sign of stress

Sleep was something I got to dread. I would snap awake, violently, every one or two hours. My body would shake within, as though it had been shot upwards from some dark, subterranean deep. Perspiration would cover my body; nauseousness and dizziness left me creeping around in slow motion, en route to the bathroom. This was when I decided to plot my nocturnal habits and sleep patterns, noting especially the frequency and rhythms of these interruptions. This pattern of interrupted sleep would continue for about six or seven days, then out of exhaustion there would be one night of sound sleep.

Try plotting your sleep patterns for one month as I did, to see if you show signs of stress.

This is how the cycle would work during a typical night:

-11:00 pm. Fall asleep with unnatural quickness
-12:30-1.30 am. Snap awake with vivid dreams. Mind racing
-4:15 am. Awake with head pressure, nausea, flushed, pulse racing
-5.30 am. Awake exhausted; bathroom trip; unable to get back to sleep

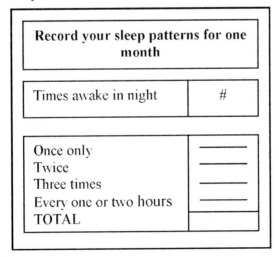

Figure 3. Recording your sleep patterns

In his book *From Stress to Strength,* Dr. Robert S. Eliot, M.D. (New York: Bantam Books, 1994), gave me the clue as to the cause of this sudden pattern of awakening after only a couple of hours. It could mean, he says, *"you are anxious and unable to control unfinished mental business."* Early morning awakening, he says, may indicate depression (page 133). I was burning out at both ends.

I had ample opportunity to apply my new breathing technique in the early hours of the morning. I would lie in bed, breathing deeply, waiting to fall back asleep. It often worked. When I was successful, even with a few hours of sleep, I felt relatively fresh in the morning. This was one of the ways I was able to conquer my broken nights. In time, I could enjoy sound refreshing sleep.

Snoring – A symptom of stress

If your spouse complains you snore louder than a broken meat grinder, as mine did, it's time you did something about it! It shocked me to learn from Carol that I was not only a chronic snorer, but a loud one.

I asked the Lord to help me find the cause of this condition. I learned that snoring is a medical condition, which has many physical causes. In my case, the Lord pointed out that my snoring and interrupted sleep patterns were the result of deep inner, unresolved stresses in my soul. As I progressed in my healing, the snoring subsided. After about a year, I was mostly free of those annoying discomforts, except for nights when stress levels were high.

Snoring occurs when airflows are obstructed in the narrow upper passages of the throat. Pressure fluctuations on the soft throat structures, the palate, tongue and uvula, cause them to vibrate. Snoring is made worse if the airways are obstructed by enlarged tonsils, adenoids or the tongue. Colds, hay fever, sinus problems will often bring on snoring. Snoring may lead to daytime drowsiness and fatigue, as mine did.

Statistics indicate that approximately 40% of adults over the age of forty, snore some or all the time, and the number is increasing.

Western, hurried lifestyles in stress foster this condition.

Sleep Apnea – A symptom of stress

I was also shocked and humbled to learn that my breathing would sometimes stop in the night! Occasionally, a "kick start" was needed to get me going again! I never found out how many times during the night this happened. All I knew was that, when it happened, it always left me drained in the morning.

This condition is known as *sleep apnea*. The medical community defines it as "*a stoppage of airflow, which lasts 5 to 10 seconds in one episode.*"

Sleep apnea is a serious medical condition, in which the back of the throat completely closes for a few seconds. As the air starts to flow again, a loud gasp, called a "*resuscitative snort*" is heard. The sufferer may move violently before falling back to sleep. Apnea severity is usually categorized by the frequency of episodes during a given night: five to fifteen episodes per hour is considered a mild form of the condition. Sleep apnea causes the heart to pump harder, even irregularly and can elevate blood pressure and enlarge the heart.

Severe interruptions of sleep like these leave one mentally and spiritually exhausted. Eight hours of sleep is essential to raise serotonin levels and to restore inner joy and vitality. But, these violent movements during sleep were sending me over the edge.

As I pondered these five areas of Stress in my life, I saw them as five storms in the making, each converging toward each other, to form the *Perfect Storm.* Had I not heeded the warning signs of these approaching storms, stress would have ultimately swept away my health.

It was humbling for me to realize these storms were all *self-inflicted*—they were all my own doing! I could have spotted them on the map before, had I paused long enough to take note. Hope came when I realized that Christ's redeeming process of SEPARATION could block the storms in their tracks, and reduce them to a cool breeze, under the control of the Holy Spirit.

It is for our freedom that Jesus died on the Cross. "*Christ has set us free to live a free life"* (Galatians 5:1 Message). It was now my turn to be free. No matter the cost, I resolved to find this freedom to increase my service to the Lord and others (Galatians 5:13).

ACTION PLAN FOR RECOVERY

I Principles

1. Finding out your susceptibility to stress through "Profiling" will give you an appreciation of its power to invade every aspect of your life; it will show you areas where *change* is needed.

2. Passivity toward *change* is a major problem in the Body of Christ. By surrendering your will to Christ, and by asking lots of questions of the Holy Spirit, a passive person will regain his power to decide.

3. Recognizing habitual behaviors as signs of unresolved stress is an important step in the de-stressing process.

II Questions

1. Self-inflicted Stress *"is more than just a body thing. It locks into the emotions and mind, and spills over onto everyone we know around us."*

   Do you see the importance of having an overall perspective of stress? Discuss with someone close to you how stress has invaded your life. How has it affected you spiritually, emotionally, mentally, physically and even socially?

2. *"The Church is filled with those who desire nothing more from Christ, other than to know they are saved. There is no will to change. Yet change or renewal is basic to the Christian life."*

   Do you agree with this statement? Are you being prompted to change? What areas do you need to change?

3. *"According to the Sleep Research Centre at Stanford University, one in four adults suffers from insomnia."*

Are you one of the four? I trust that you have already tracked your sleep patterns. If you are experiencing broken sleep, it is time to ask the Lord the reasons why. Psalm 127:2 says that the Lord *"gives (blessings) to His beloved in sleep."* And you, my friend, are His beloved!

III Prayer

Father, You are so good! Thank You for opening my eyes to see the potential storm that has been gathering all around me. I have been totally unaware that it was a storm of my own making. Please forgive me for not seeing this before. There are many areas of my life which need to be changed. I give them all to You. (Be specific). *I give You permission to change me. I want to walk in Your peace. Please give me the grace to SEPARATE out every stressor in my life. I pray this in the name of Jesus Christ, my Lord and Savior. Amen.*

CHAPTER THREE

The workings of stress in your body

"My people are destroyed for lack of knowledge."
(Hosea 4:6)

Getting to know the workings of stress in our bodies is vital for walking continuously in Christ's peace. Knowledge is a powerful weapon against the enemy. It is the wise that lay up this kind of knowledge (Proverbs 10:14a).

Medical science is beginning to unravel the mysteries of how stress impacts the brain and our immune systems. The process is complex and opinions vary. The ideas presented below are meant to introduce this technical subject as a base for your knowledge of stress. This overview is not meant to be exhaustive or definitive, but an outline, flexible enough to cope with changing theories.

HOW THE BRAIN TALKS!

In Eden, Adam enjoyed a free flow of intuitive, instructive, love-filled thoughts, which flowed from his Creator every day. Like David, he could have said: *"How precious also are thy thoughts unto me, O God! How great is the sum of them!"* (Psalm 139: 17 KJV). Adam's pace of receiving and thinking was at the optimum speed for life on earth.

Getting to know the workings of stress in our bodies is vital for walking continuously in Christ's peace.

Our brains are like that of Adam's! We process thousands of thoughts and impressions each day. God designed a unique system of transforming our thoughts into brain chemicals, so that the brain cells can speak to each other. These brain chemicals act as *messengers*. They interact between the trillions of brain cells every day, creating a constant chatter in their strange language.

A single thought or impression is all it takes to activate these brain chemicals. They respond not only to what we think, but also to what we imagine and feel. It makes no difference if the thoughts are generated from real live events, or from imaginations in the mind, the *messengers* still flow between the cells.

What happens when our body needs extra energy?

When we need extra bursts of energy and strength, for running or lifting, or a disciplined mental exercise, the need is first registered in the mind. This need activates the brain chemicals and the hormonal system of the body. The heart rate, blood pressure, and glucose levels are then increased to the required levels. When the need passes, the system is restored to balance. Peace reigns in the body.

God knew in His wisdom how we would need such a built-in restorative balancing system to help us through our days.

In Medical Science, this arrangement is known as the *homeostatic mechanism,* which fine tunes and balances our brain activities to our body needs.

This homeostatic mechanism operates by way of *"happy messengers,"* which are chemicals possessing natural tranquillizing abilities. *Serotonin* is one important brain chemical classed as a "Happy Hormone." Serotonin slows our thinking, making us feel relaxed in stressful times. Production of this neurotransmitter is known to increase measurably even when we think or do acts of kindness. Even a smile sent out to another is known to raise a person's serotonin level!

The prophet Isaiah indicated the secret of maintaining a peaceful brain, with its chemicals flowing between cells in balance: *"You will guard him and keep him in perfect and constant peace whose MIND IS STAYED ON YOU* (Isaiah 26:3 Emphasis added.). No wonder Paul advises we keep Scripture and Psalms running through our minds as much as possible (Ephesians 5:19).

Other "happy chemicals" include *Melatonin,* which helps maintain good sleep patterns; *Dopamine* regulates pleasure and reduces pain; *Adrenaline* and its cousin *Noradrenaline,* are needed for higher energy levels.

Some of these tranquillizing hormones are said to be as powerful as morphine. All provide a remarkable protective system that keeps our minds and bodies in harmony. Without this *homeostatic mechanism* in our brains operating continually, we would be in a constant high state of alarm, pain and tiredness!

Knowing these facts provided an added incentive for me to keep calm in stressful situations.

The "heart" as a 'command' centre

There is good reason why God placed the heart in the centre of the body. He designed this organ to respond to all stimuli we receive from the world, the flesh, and the devil. All physical, emotional and mental and spiritual activity is registered in the heart. Everything we do, think or say is monitored by this unique organ. Whether pride, fear, shame, guilt, or peace, love, or joy, the heart registers their messages. Our heart constantly mirrors the health of our spirit, soul, and body, as well as our stress levels.

Stress starts in the head but it is the heart that instantly responds.

There is good reason why God placed the heart in the centre of our body. He designed this organ to respond to all stimuli we

receive from the world, the
flesh, and the devil.

The heart is far more than a mere pump. It is a highly sensitive organ, with an intelligence of its own. As Dr. Archibald Hart, in his book *Adrenaline and Stress* tells us, it *"is a genius organ"* which thinks for itself!

Our circulatory system, he says, is a vast irrigation system, centered about this unique pump. *"Every day the heart pumps about 2000 gallons of blood,(the equivalent to a hundred large automobile gas tanks) through 60,000 miles of elastic tubing"*(page 19*)*. In one life span of 72 years, it pumps some 25 billion times! Trillions of body cells are fed through its intricate system of minute canals. Body fluids stream through these canals in a gentle, steady flow, reaching every cell. The problem is, the canals clog with waste products of metabolism. Drainage slows and body problems begin to develop, all of which inform the heart.

Dr. Jay Cohn, head of the cardio-vascular division, University of Minnesota Medical School, also supports this notion that the heart is a key responder to all internal and external stimuli. When we get nervous or excited, or when someone scares us, our hearts immediately respond in rate, force, and contraction. These hearts of ours are remarkably sensitive to even micro changes in our thinking. Truly, we *are "fearfully and wonderfully made!"* (Psalms 139:14 KJV).

Jesus said as much 2000 years ago! He spoke only to the "hearts" of men, never to their intellect. He saw how men had patterned their thinking based on the influences of the world, the flesh, and the devil, and how it made men insensitive to His Word. Stress was then able to work in them unimpeded. They had ignored the promptings of their heart to exchange their thinking for His peace and paid the price in stress.

This then, is how stress begins! It starts in the mind with a worry about our job, church, our spouse, family, friends, unpaid bills, or the robbery next door. Worry is transformed into chemicals, which bombard this life-giving organ—the heart, with fiery messages conveying worrisome thoughts and stressful images. There is no natural resistance to this daily onslaught—only a spiritual one.

In this raging fire, our happy hormones are hard-pressed to keep us in peace and harmony. As the homeostatic mechanism shifts out of balance, our minds then start to race, the heart works harder, blood pressure and sugar levels are raised, and the receptors in the muscles tighten our limbs. We are charged for fight or flight. But, it is a condition that is all self-inflicted!

Stress works silently, impacting the heart and body without our being aware of its actions. When we see the role of the brain and heart in stress, the progressive development of stress is easier to understand.

THE STAGES OF STRESS

Pastor Henry Wright, in his book The *More Excellent Way*, Pleasant Valley Publications, Thomaston, Georgia, 2000, (page 152) outlines three stages in the progression of a stress cycle. There are no definite boundaries between each stage.

Stage I – THE ALARM STAGE

We have already seen that normal living, places occasional heavy demands upon the body for extra energy. Production of chemical messengers is temporarily thrown out of kilter. In more detail, this is how the system works when we are alarmed or frightened by a sudden change in our circumstances.

A bear in your back garden will likely fill your mind with fear-filled thoughts and trigger the onset of the Alarm Stage. Your thoughts are instantly picked up by the hypothalamus, a gland located at the back of your head. This is where "*tension*" begins. It is why we subconsciously reach to massage this area of our necks, to relieve muscular tightness. The hypothalamus immediately informs the heart to prepare for flight or fight!

The hypothalamus gland is said to be the "*brain*" of the endocrine system. It responds to the barrage of fear-filled thoughts received in the brain by writing a chemical prescription for a powerful complex of hormones known as *catecholamines*. These chemical messengers provide us with options on how we should deal with the danger of the bear. Among those released into the blood stream are the stimulants adrenaline and its cousin nora-drenaline in copious amounts.

According to Dr. Eliot (ibid, page 23), these emergency hormones provide the initial extra energy to fight the intruder, and the rising feelings of anxiety. As the stress event unfolds its dangers, fear may progress to anger in an impulse to fight the beast, and then noradrenaline is released. These catecholamines may save your life in the short run, but their prolonged surgings will kill you in the end.

If the danger increases, the "brain" signals the pituitary, thyroid, adrenals and other hormone-producing glands into producing more stress chemicals. They work together, stimulating the heart to pump harder under the stress, raising blood pressure levels, increasing cholesterol and sending glucose to the muscles, all to prepare the body for its fight or flight decisions.

These reactions take place simultaneously—in a nanosecond in the body-all from a few fearful thoughts in the mind!

Temporarily the body's hormonal system is thrown out of balance. Once the danger is passed, the homeostatic mechanism restores the hormonal system back to its former optimum levels of performance. We sense the peace around our heart once again.

The body's natural tranquillizers, stimulants and pain killers, therefore, act initially as anti-stress, combat soldiers on the front line, calming our anxieties and fears. But they are for short-term assignments only.

Stage II – THE RESISTANCE STAGE (GENERAL ADAPTATION STAGE)

This stage begins when the body is unable to return to normal and must adapt to more permanent higher stress levels. The onslaught of invading fear stressors keeps the hypothalamus in overdrive, commanding the pituitary and adrenal cortex into pump-ing out more of their hormones, notably adrenaline and cortisol.

Minor discomforts began to appear as my body bathed more and more in these harmful hormones. Shifting pain told me that something was going wrong. Sudden bouts of extreme fatigue and nausea would overtake me. But I saw no need to cut back on my workloads, or take inventory of my life.

Unknown to me, as my anxiety feelings intensified, my body became addicted to these adrenaline rushes in order to maintain my fast-paced lifestyle.

As the natural tranquillizers in my body depleted, a pervasive sense of hopelessness and despair tried to take over. I was feeling more and more fragile and brittle, with the smallest incident almost sending me over the cliff. At times, my mind raced with confusing, meaningless patterns of thought that wouldn't shut down. At other times, it was as though my mind fogged, or simply numbed out. This brought on the fear that *"I was losing it!"*

Hidden, prickly rivers coursed through my legs, arms, and shoulders all day long. This sensation was often accompanied by great heat. I thought it was my heart! I didn't know it at the time, but this was adrenaline preparing me for flight or fight. Before long, these constant chemical baths began to affect my entire body. When the surges were prolonged my pulse bounded. Cramps would also affect my feet and hands; sore throats, canker sores, colds, minor infections and pressure headaches became more frequent. I learned to recognize these "rushes" as the precursors to full-blown, anxiety-panic attacks.

Carol and I continued to minister to others, even as my stress level began to build. This was the stage when my blood pressure began to rise slowly, with systolic blood pressure levels rising into the 120-145 range, spiking occasionally well over 200. Cholesterol levels rose to 7.4.

Dr. Eliot mentions that in this stage of stress, vital chemicals, such as sodium are retained; metabolism drops and gastric acid flows increase; high energy fats are released into the blood stream; energy is diverted from our immune system; and non-essentials such as the production of sex hormones are suppressed.

During my final visit to the emergency room, prescriptions for anti-depressants were recommended. They are known as SSRI's (Selective Serotonin Reuptake Inhibitors), which work to curb racing minds and erratic thinking. They are designed to manage serotonin levels in the brain, helping to bridge nerve junctions or synapses, promoting or suppressing flows of brain chemicals between nerve cells. Zoloff, Effexor, Paxil and Luvox are among those widely used. None of them actually stimulates natural serotonin production.

Stage III – THE EXHAUSTION STAGE

Short-term perks may enable us to run on *"highs"* for a period, but over the longer term, the heart will eventually respond with signals to slow down. When we disobey God, men's hearts fail in fear (Luke 21:26 KJV). The body is no longer able to resist the tormenting stressors of fear and starts to shut down.

The body enters the third stage of the cycle—exhaustion—which is normally the result of years of stress build-up. It builds in the body until it is ready to explode! Is it any surprise that since 1981, there has been a 353% increase in prescriptions for anti-depressants in Canada (The *Globe & Mail,* Nov 2, 2002)?

As the anxiety and worry deepened in me, dark, heavy foreboding thoughts began to overshadow my days, as though something terrible was about to happen. After each anxiety attack, feelings of gloom would ride over me in waves. Depression would last for about two days. Bouts of extreme fatigue became more frequent. There was no let-up in the hormonal surges in my legs and arms. Head pressures made me dizzy. Even more terrifying were the sudden memory blanks in my mind. When I tried to recall something, instead of another thought, an empty blackness confronted me. It was though I had lost a part of my mind! Even my dreams became nightmarish.

It was clear that my immune system had become affected. Minor infections and ailments multiplied and seemed to take long periods to heal. As the pressure beneath my chest tightened, fears of heart problems plagued my mind; I also thought I had an advanced prostate problem. I found out later that stress will mimic failure in these areas.

Recognizing the symptoms and understanding the mechanisms of stress working in my body lifted a great deal of the fear associated with the unknowns of Stress. Knowledge gave me hope that, with God's help, I could find the wisdom to manage this condition and receive healing.

I trust that this section has encouraged you to keep on and not to give up. You ARE on the right track in your journey out of stress.

ACTION PLAN FOR RECOVERY

I Principles

1. **Stress works silently** in the body, without our being aware of the symptoms. Gradually, it takes over every part of us. But at the centre of its activities is the heart, urging us to do something about it! Knowledge of the process is vital for personal health, and well being. Without this knowledge, God's people are perishing.

2. **Stress starts in the mind.** Toxic emotions and thoughts are transformed into dangerous chemicals, which circulate through the brain and body organs.

3. **Recognition** of stress symptoms and understanding of the mechanisms of stress removes fear from us. It gives us hope that with God's help, we will acquire the wisdom to manage stress and receive healing.

II Questions

1. *"A single thought is all it takes to activate these brain chemicals, which respond not only to what we think, but also to what we imagine and feel. It makes no difference if the thoughts are generated from real live events, or from the imaginations of the mind, the messengers still flow between the cells."*

Did you know that your body responds automatically to what you feel and think? It is unable to distinguish between reality and the unreal, the truth or a lie. Can you see how important it is to SEPARATE out every negative emotion and thought and to change them? Why not start now to write them down?

2. *"According to Dr. Eliot (ibid, page 23), adrenaline provides needed extra energy when we are anxious; noradrenaline is*

released later, as the stress event unfolds its danger, and when emotions progress from fear to anger in the impulse to fight the beast."

Do you take your hormonal system for granted? Have you ever considered how it affects you in stressful situations?

III Prayer

Father, I acknowledge that You are the One who created me with a carefully balanced hormonal system. I realize now that by allowing my emotions free reign, I have abused my own body. I have never considered before how harmful stress hormones worked, and how sickness results if they are not brought back into balance. Holy Spirit, help me acquire the kind of knowledge I need about stress, how it works in my body, emotions, and mind. Thank You, Lord Jesus. Amen.

CHAPTER FOUR

Managing your stress

"Blessed is the man... whom You discipline...
that You may give him power to keep himself calm
in the days of adversity."
(Psalms 94:12-13)

B ecoming aware of stress symptoms in your body and taking responsibility for them, is the first step toward healing. The aim, for all of us, is to reduce the intensity of our symptoms before starting to deal with their hidden causes. Making the decision to eliminate or control this nuisance inevitably means radical changes in daily schedules, attitudes, habits, and behavior.

Here are a few of the changes I implemented to manage the physical aspects of my stress. I trust they will help you come out of your S.I.S. They work! But we need to try them and to keep at them.

My nurse tutor began with a lesson on breathing. That's where we begin.

1. BREATHE DEEPER FOR LONGER LIFE!

We are air machines. God designed the nostrils to receive the air we breathe. Adam was given the Spirit of Life through his nose! *"The Lord...breathed into his nostrils the breath or spirit of life;*

and man became a living being" (Genesis 2: 7). The word "breath" *naphach* (#5301 Strong's Concordance) means in Hebrew to inflate, blow hard! Even Job recognized this truth: *"while my breath is in me and the Spirit of God is in my nostrils..."* (Job 27:3, KJV*).

But we have adapted to our smog-filled, polluted atmosphere, by subconsciously breathing shallow—mostly through the mouth. Our sedentary lifestyles don't help, either. Stress builds in us without any resistance!

The air we breathe is not only polluted, but is impoverished of essential life elements. Fossil amber tells a remarkably sorry tale of this change. Bubbles of air, trapped in fossil amber were found to contain as much as 38% oxygen, which promoted a luxurious forest growth evident for one period of geologic time. Today, we breathe air with an oxygen content of 18-20% and it is going lower, especially in the cities. To compensate, we tend to breathe more rapidly, with fears that our air is poisonous.

If a person doesn't get enough fresh air, or is a shallow breather, the oxygen intake doesn't remove the toxic gases out of his body. Oxygen is designed as one of nature's best detoxifiers. Deep breathing releases carbon dioxide waste from the body cells, stimulates the brain cells, and quickens the memory.

We are air machines. Oxygen is designed as one of nature's best detoxifiers.

In his book *The Miracle of Fasting* (California: Health Science, page 147), Paul C. Bragg discovered a common denominator to long-living people. They were all deep breathers! He found that those who took fewer, but deeper breaths, in one minute, lived the longest! Most rapid breathers are short-lived. Paul Bragg practiced long slow, deep-breathing exercises, first in the morning, and then several times a day. This is what we should do. Shallow breathing restricts the amount of oxygen required for the bloodstream.

Seniors especially fail to see the importance of deep breathing. The result is a cluster of symptoms relating to anxiety and panic:

fatigue, gas, insomnia, muscle cramps.

One doctor informed me that hyperventilation, in times of anxiety attacks, needs to be understood as a breathing problem. The natural tendency of the body under intense stress is to take shallow, gasping breaths through the mouth. This is the wrong way! This simple breathing exercise was given to me by the nurse, which I repeat here for you:

> *"When you feel stressed,"* she said *"take slow deep breaths, filling your body cavity until it will hold no more, and then allow your breath to be exhaled slowly through the mouth. Breathe through the nose, keeping your mouth lightly closed. Visualize the healing air entering your body. As you breathe, allow your stomach muscles to relax. Hold for a few seconds; then breathe out slowly, through pursed lips."*

She suggested also fixing your mind on a pleasant scene, or a person. For a Christian, the obvious would be Jesus Christ. As you gaze upon Him, visualize all tension leaving your body. As you repeat this exercise, ask God to release the toxins from every cell and then notice how relaxed you feel.

Sam Graci, in his book the *Power of Superfoods* (Scarborough, Ontario: Prentice Hall, 1999, page 166) recommends this same exercise, lying on your back. He also suggests a type of purification breathing, through one nostril at a time. Stop your right nostril with the first finger, while releasing your left nostril with the thumb. When breathing is alternated from one nostril to the other, you'll find it very calming; leaving you with the feeling you have conquered stress. It takes only two or three minutes, and should be practiced first thing in the morning before an open window. Practicing this simple exercise will re-tone your stressed-out body, and bring you into a deeper rest at night. I used this method many times to bring down my adrenaline levels.

Deep breathing is vital to body health and longer life. If you are exercising, combine them with deep invigorating inhales and exhales. It will turn your body into a virtual fat burning machine.

2. DRINK WATER – LOTS OF IT!

Stress accelerates water loss from the body. But we are too preoccupied to notice! A dry mouth, fatigue, and headaches are commonly known symptoms of dehydration, but they are also symptoms of a stressed-out body. Had I known this, I might have saved myself from a good deal of discomfort.

Drinking water by the glassful, one after another, first thing in the morning, was never an alternative to a good mug of coffee! Since my last hospital visit, I have changed my morning routine in favor of water. Water does reduce stress levels. Two 8 oz glasses of good water in the morning before breakfast and six or more during the course of the day, flushes out the toxins and maintains good health.

As we age, the mechanisms in our body, which tell us we must drink water, gradually shut down. This is why chronic dehydration is a problem among seniors. The body goes into drought management. Keeping our body hydrated is one of the best ways not only to manage stress, but also to maintain body health.

De-stressing with smart water

Drinking municipal tap water, unfiltered well water, even bottled water, should throw up cautions. This water may contain undesirable chemicals, and occasional harmful contaminants, including Giardia, Cryptosporidium, E-coli, volatile organic compounds and metals. The pH reading may be acid. In addition, the molecular structure of most drinking water is clustered with the molecules being large. This prevents ready absorption of the water into the cells of the body.

Carol and I had many failed attempts to find the right kind of water for our health needs. We finally decided upon a high-tech water maker, which not only draws water through several filters, but also changes the molecular structure of the water. The body hydrates, or absorbs the water faster than tap water and makes the water more digestible. The pH is raised to 7.4, which is slightly alkaline. With this water, we found it easy to drink six to eight 8-oz glasses each day. We found it also to be a great de-stressor and great health giver.

3. EXERCISE TO BREAK STRESS

Heart smart exercises are powerful de-stressors and an important aid to longevity. Exercise builds positive mental attitudes, fortifies the will power, and promotes efficiency. You will not only feel better, but you will look younger! *"Satisfying the body's craving for physical activity produces the miraculous feeling of agelessness and youthfulness"* (Bragg, page 184).

> ## Vigorous exercise, three times a week will keep your stress level in check, and help you enjoy life better.

Deterioration of the body quickly sets in without a careful exercise regime. The body becomes flabby and susceptible to all manner of ailments. If you don't have time for exercise, you'd better reserve lots of time for sickness. Vigorous exercise three times a week will keep your stress level in check, and help you enjoy life more. Aim to gradually raise your heart rate during your workout, which will drive oxygen to every part of your body. Oxygenating your body will restore your health.

Here are some ideas we incorporated into a weekly exercise regime:

Speed walking: Speed walking is the king of all exercises and is good for everyone. Walking fast is one of the best ways to absorb oxygen, and burn fat. Walking tones all our body systems simultaneously, including the brain. Drink two glasses of your preferred water at room temperature before your breakfast and then walk. Start slowly. Build up to 30-45 minutes of fast-paced walking at 4 miles per hour. Try to raise your pulse rate.

Walking brings harmony to the central nervous system. Graci (ibid, page 155) points out that walking is a contra lateral movement. We learn this coordination of alternate swinging of arms and legs as toddlers. But as we age, we lose this ability—walking becomes more of a shuffle. Deliberately cultivating arm-swinging in walking will revitalize the body's sense of coordination and balance. You feel immediately refreshed and energized.

Morning exercise is best. Your resting metabolic rate (RMR) will greatly improve with regular physical activity. Set goals. If you walk 6+ miles per week, this would translate into roughly 300 miles in one year. If you do reach such a goal, give yourself a big star in your logbook!

In any case, warm up for the first five or ten minutes, then go for it! Try a 5-minute burst, once every quarter-hour, walking as fast as you can, then drop back to a slower rate. If you are out of doors, change your route frequently to add interest.

Lift Weights: For those older, the idea of weightlifting might seem too radical, even dangerous. Most would doubt the wisdom of even trying. But in a study undertaken by the U.S. Government, in the Human Nutrition Research Center on aging, at Tufts University in Boston, aged nursing home residents were asked to pump iron! The results were astonishing! Frail residents, ages 86-96, were able to triple and quadruple their muscle strength in a matter of a few weeks (Bragg, ibid, page 185).

The study director, Dr. M.A. Fiatarone, closely supervised the weight-lifting program, emphasizing safety and regularity, even among those with known terminal illnesses. No serious medical problems resulted from the program, only benefits!

Muscle weakness and atrophy are a common sign of premature aging, especially in the over fifties. There are 640 muscles in the body. Disuse causes muscles to drop!

Pumping iron works the main muscle groups, and strengthens the heart. If you are over fifty, a trainer at a recognized fitness studio is recommended. Consistent weight resistant exercises are a must if you want to fight stress. Carol and I began with small weights at home. Our regime was brief, about fifteen minutes, but we noticed a difference. We then joined an Athletic Club, and within a few months, our muscle tone improved tremendously. We could push and pull with ease! We were less tired and could better withstand falls and shocks to the body. Resistance to disease was

greater, and recovery from minor ailments was faster. Our cholesterol levels lowered, and Carol's bone density greatly improved!

4. DE-STRESS YOUR BRAIN WITH NUTRIENTS

Communication in the brain is by way of electro-chemical
nerve impulses. Our brain requires constant nutrient support to
build these chemicals. In severe stress, the brain uses large quantities of brain nutrients manufactured by the nerve cells.

Modern diets are generally unable to supply the needed raw
materials for their manufacture in the brain nerve cells. To offset
this lack, the Natural Health Industry has identified a number of
nutrients, which are already being marketed to help sufferers with
anxiety disorders.

These natural supplements are now available in health stores,
providing "brain food" for us in the management of stress. These
supplements replace depleted metabolites in the brain through
single component capsules or patented complex formulations.
Studies show that individuals taking multivitamins and mineral
supplements experience less anxiety.

The "B" family is especially important: B6-(pyridoxine) is
required for the manufacture of serotonin (50-100 mg daily), along
with vitamin C; Bananas and turkey will help keep serotonin levels
up; B12-(cobalamin) is essential for nerve cell metabolism, and is a
fatigue fighter (50-200 mg.daily). Other nutrients include L-
glutamine, a nutritional supplement, as found in certain fish (mack-
erel). Vitamin A (fish liver oil, carrots); chromium (shell fish and
corn oil), and calcium are used in concentrated form in supplements.

A common mineral deficiency in stressed-out people is magnesium, which helps to maintain inner calm, and our ability to think
clearly. I found *magnesium oxide* to be very helpful in stressful
times, often taking one tablet just before sleep. Another micronutri-
ent is *GABA (gamma amino butyric acid)*, a natural inhibitor, which
is often found to be deficient in anxiety patients. Low GABA
reduces adrenaline output, but results in quickening emotional
responses, like anger, especially during Phase II of the stress cycle.
GABA is unavailable in Canada. As a supplement, Janet Maccaro

gives GABA high marks. I found, however, that GABA, in the dose recommended, resulted in some uncomfortable sensations. Melatonin supplement is helpful in restoring sleep.

In rare cases of prolonged stress, the body will eat itself if it is starving for nutrients. In its attempt to restore hormonal balance, and maintain production of brain chemicals, the body will pull nutrients from certain organs of the body to fill the deficit. For example, the skin organ may blotch white, like a leper, spreading in an unsightly way over the arms, chest and legs. If there is no drug therapy or radical alteration of lifestyle, with major changes to work and mental habits, this drain of vital elements on the organs will render the body vulnerable to viral attacks, and degenerative diseases.

In severe stress, the brain uses large quantities of brain chemicals, manufactured by the nerve cells.

If you are strong in your desire to fight your self-inflicted stressors, changing your lifestyle with nutrient-wellness regimes is a must. Stay away from, or cut back on 'mood foods' such as salt, sugar, alcohol and caffeine. In excess, they will influence your stress level. Try going 75-80% raw fruit and vegetables for each meal of the day and notice how well you will feel within days.

5. AIM TO BE DRUG FREE

Our family doctor gave me the option of prescription drugs as the best alternative for my anxiety problems. He recommended common antidepressants, such as Prozac, Ridlin, or Atavan. It seemed all too convenient.

No wonder depression anxiety is a multibillion dollar industry with our younger generation being the most drug dependent group in history.

I was informed of the risks: success with antidepressant drugs are well documented, but the potential side effects are a serious deterrent. Prozac, for example, induces nausea; Xanac, mild amnesia and reduced physical coordination. Some SSRI's may kindle suicidal tendencies. Withdrawals from some SSRI's are also known to create periods of severe body, emotional, and mental reactions.

I tried to juggle my beliefs as a child of God with those of the medical establishment. As a pastor I felt vulnerable, walking on a thin edge. I had often preached that *"He (Jesus) heals the broken-hearted and binds up their wounds (curing their pains and their sorrows)"* (Psalms 147:3). This is a promise that can never be broken. Jesus is able to restore our health and heal our wounds (Jeremiah 30: 17). But did I really believe it now? Would the rock of His Word turn to sand after months, even years, of waiting for my healing?

If I did fill their prescriptions, how would I handle the inevitable guilt of being unable to stand on His Word? The Apostle Paul makes it clear *"... therefore (there is) now no condemnation (no adjudging guilty of wrong) for those who are in Christ Jesus, who live (and) walk not after the dictates of the flesh, but after the dictates of the Spirit"* (Romans 8:1).

Many Christians I know are able to function as servants in the Body of Christ, even in leadership, medicated for depression or anxiety without feelings of guilt. Would I experience this same grace?

Al's addictive patterns started when he was a youngster. He tried to bury the shame of being abandoned by his dad, whom he worshipped. Rejection had wounded his spirit and fears of being rejected again worked as a silent enemy within him. In his attempt to nullify the guilt and anger towards his dad, Al rebelled first in habitual swearing; later, in his teens, he added smoking and alcohol. By the time he was twenty, he was addicted to hard, street drugs.

When he confessed Christ as his Savior he gave up street drugs, but his doctor prescribed pharmaceutical drugs to numb his body pain. The patterns of thought creating the need for drugs in the first place were still there! He still felt rejected and wounded. The abandoned child in him still craved love and affection from his dad. His guilt and anger, although buried, were still very much alive. They surfaced every time he felt hurt. His wound still bled! Permanent healing was impossible for him, until he submitted his mind to God. *"When I get rid of the pain within me, I won't need drugs"* he said to me. He had to become responsible for his own thoughts and attitudes before he could receive his emotional healing. Gradually, Al realized that God's best was that he be without drugs. When he released his rejection, anger, resentment and guilt to God in forgiveness, God's grace was there to meet his need. Through confession and FORGIVENESS he was set totally free from addictive thinking patterns and from the cravings in his body for drugs. He then went on to serve the Lord in ministry.

Taking prescription drugs might also induce a dependency I didn't need. I found no credible evidence that drug therapy could do anything more than cap buried hurts in the soul. They may alleviate physical symptoms of stress, but cannot unravel tangled emotions, and destructive thought patterns locked up in the subconscious mind. They cannot locate hidden anger, hate and roots of unforgiveness. Even a six-month therapy regime on drugs, if it worked, could inoculate my will against seeking any further deliverance from the pain in my soul.

I decided against taking drugs, but the decision wasn't easy. I could have caved in to the temptation many times. But I thank the Lord for His grace that enabled me to trust Him without reservation.

I pray that you will take this time to search out the path that Jesus has personally designed for your way out of stress. He delights to take us from where we are to where He wants us to be in Him.

6. LET YOUR DREAMS HELP YOU

I first stumbled on the value of dreams during my own periods of stress-crisis. I realized that the bizarre colouramas of my nightly watchings were bringing messages from the subconscious about the condition of my soul.

Vivid, often ugly, high drama is the soul's way of getting our attention. Otherwise, we would miss the messages they convey. While many dreams process mental junk, taken into the mind during the course of the day, training the soul and spirit to sift them out will turn your dream world into an important tool for guiding you through stress. Dreams are often God's way of informing and instructing us of soulish pressures needing our immediate attention.

Western society has lost the wonder of dreams. We see them as irrelevant in our high tech, fast-paced lives—even cultic. Our needs are met from the enormous resources in the world. These nocturnal interruptions are meaningless, even a nuisance. They inflict, more often than not, downers on our day. But within this cacophony of our dream world lie important truths we need to find.

Dreams are voices of the world, the flesh, the devil, and God. The question is—who's talking?

Worldly influences impact our dreams, encouraging us or even warning us of its dangers. *Fleshly* dreams are the smoke effluent of a soul burning out its excesses. Its desires and cravings jostle for supremacy in our dream world. *Devilish* dreams shoot poison arrows into our minds, especially during sleep. He targets our weak passive areas to pull us down. Dreams emanating from the *Spirit* are the best. They are often accompanied by a wonderful sense of Christ's peace. *God* tries to get through to us, imparting Wisdom through our spirit in vivid, colorful, often three-part dreams. God uses them to guide, instruct and inform of things to come.

> **For believers in Jesus Christ, dreams can be a vital tool. With practice, we may discover their hidden messages.**

Get to know the symbols and meanings of your dreams. A hotel, for example, is a place of temporary rest. A mall is a place of variety and abundance. Common sense should always be your guide. A hot revved-up car, driving over the speed limit in a downtown crowded area, was one of my oft-repeated dreams. It conveyed a warning: Slow down or you will burn out and even crash! For believers in Jesus Christ, dreams can be vital message carriers; with practice you will discover their hidden messages.

As they come, jot down their main elements before you go back to sleep or when you get up. Otherwise, they will be gone! You will be amazed at their ability to guide you into prayer.

Habakkuk recorded his visions and Christians should do the same. We should ponder them, searching for patterns and clues.

Sarah, a teen, came to us tearful and very distressed. She had been a Christian for a number of years and was a member of her church worship team. For several nights in a row she had experienced terrible nightmares, which she interpreted to be an omen of her impending, violent death. *"Charles Manson was coming at me with a knife. I couldn't get away from him. I was terrified."*

As we listened to her story, we at that time had no idea that dreams had any significance to a person's mental health. We kept calm, wondering if this was a little out of our depth. We asked God to intervene in one of those classically sophisticated prayers that breaks open heavens gates: *"Help!"*

We asked Sarah to list all the emotions she had experienced in just one of her dreams. Then we asked her if she had ever felt these same emotions, as a package, earlier in her life. Without hesitation she said yes. *"It was when my dad announced to the family that he was leaving. I tried to get in between my mom and dad. It was like I was being divided, cut in half. I was so angry at my dad; I hated him."*

So here were all the elements of stress hidden away in her young heart. For ten years, all the judgments, the hatred toward her dad, and the expectations that it would happen again, festered like an open sore in her soul. Several times her expectations were fulfilled when those closest to her had suddenly been taken from her in freak accidents and sicknesses. A knife had cut deep scars in her soul with each loss. After we brought these judgments and hatred toward her dad to the Cross, the enormous weight of guilt lifted from her. God had been waiting all along to bring healing to her tormented mind. She was never troubled this way again.

At the peak of one of my panic attacks, I dreamt of a sinewy, black stallion, kicking and rearing up in a mad frenzy. He was imprisoned atop a high, barren plateau. But there was no way down; the cliff faces were too steep. I looked into his bulging, black eyes, filled with fire and terror. The stallion longed to be free. It was a graphic illustration of me trapped in the fury of an anxiety attack. As my healing progressed, my dreams became more peaceful, instructive and helpful.

A note of caution with regard to dream interpretation: There are many books on the market now listing dream symbols and their meanings. Most of these books tap into spiritual darkness. If you intend to pursue this field, make sure you find good Christian resources to guide you, for example at Streams Ministries International, North Sutton, New Hampshire, USA.

ACTION PLAN FOR RECOVERY

I Principles

1. We were designed as air machines! Taking note of how you breathe is essential for lowering your stress levels and maintaining good health.

2. Drinking water, 6-8 glasses (8 oz), of the right kind, especially first thing in the morning, will help revitalize your body and reduce stress.

3. Exercise is also a powerful de-stressor. A regular weekly regime is a must to lower stress levels and is important if you desire a long healthy life.

II Questions

1. *"If a person doesn't get enough fresh air, or is a shallow breather, the oxygen intake doesn't remove the toxic gases in his body."*

Have you ever taken note of how you breathe during the course of a day? If you are a shallow breather, the best remedy is to begin your mornings breathing deeply with fresh air, filling your body cavity to the bottom. Notice how invigorated you feel. In times of stress, practice the breathing techniques given in this chapter.

2. *"Deterioration of the body quickly sets in without a careful exercise program."*

If you are not already involved in a weekly exercise regime, you should consider such a program, if you intend keeping your stress levels at manageable levels. Write down some practical goals for an exercise program and aim for a specific time to start!

3. *"Dreams are voices of the world, the flesh, the devil, and God. The question is—who's talking"?*

When so many voices come at us during sleep, do you see the importance of SEPARATING them out? Pray into your dreams, and ask the Holy Spirit to help you discern the Truths He wants you to hear.

III Prayer

Father, I realize now that I have been lax in the way I have cared for my body. As a result, I have allowed stress to build in many areas. Please forgive me. Give me the strength to change my daily routine and to incorporate the suggestions of this chapter into my life. I know I must lower my stress levels, and I see that this is the way to do it. Help me also to understand my dreams and to bring them under the management of the Holy Spirit. Thank You, Lord Jesus. Amen.

CHAPTER FIVE

Linking stress to sickness

Job with loathsome and painful sores (boils) says,
*"I will not restrain my mouth; I will speak in the anguish of
my spirit. I will complain in the bitterness of my soul... You
scare me with dreams and terrify me through visions so that
I would choose strangling and death, rather than these my
bones. I loathe my life."*
(Job 7: 11-15)

If we fail to manage our stress symptoms, then stress will begin to manage us! The gate then opens wide for sicknesses to appear. SEPARATION of all our stressors is a necessary part of healing.

You must have noticed how a cold affects every part of you. It pulls you down. You feel miserable; your thoughts race or freeze, and your nerves feel raw. And you don't want to see anyone. Body, soul, and spirit are inextricably bound to each other.

Job was under great stress because he worried so much about his children. His stressed-out emotions became a foothold for the devil to work on his body with unsightly skin eruptions. Job failed to see the link between his sickness and the multiplying stress factors in his life. His emotions, attitudes on life, his speech, and sleep patterns were all out of kilter. The root of his physical problem was not in a boil virus, but in the toxic patterns of his soulish emotions and thinking. He had allowed his life to fill with fear.

If someone suggested to you that your cholesterol and heart problems related to your feelings and thought patterns, you, no doubt, would be upset. You might even snap back: *"What I feel or think has nothing to do with my sickness!"* Yet the opposite is true. This is a concept, which is now being accepted by a widening body in medical and natural health research. We really do perish for lack of knowledge. The devil has blinded our eyes to this truth.

There exists an invisible link between what we think and the health of our bodies.

Prior to the Fall, Adam's health in the Garden was perfect. His spirit dominated, harmonizing his soul to his body. The Fall reversed this order. Instead of his *spirit* being dominant, his *body* emerged as king! From that time on, mankind followed in Adam's footsteps. We delight in pampering, feeding, and protecting our bodies, especially when they are sick. But we ignore the flashing signals that prompt us to change the way we express our feelings and our minds.

In James Allen's classic, *As a Man Think*eth (California: DeVoss & Company), he says: *"Sickly thoughts will express themselves through a sickly body. Thoughts of fear have been known to kill a man as speedily as a bullet."* We are unfamiliar with the way we think; we are unable to see how aches in the head, shoulders and stomach connect to deadly thought-bullets shooting across our minds.

In recent years, the pioneering works of Christian researchers, notably John and Paula Sandford, Dr. Ed Smith, Dr. Grant Mullen, Joyce Meyer, and Pastor Henry Wright have underscored this connection between stressed-out emotions and thinking to sickness. We are now learning to SEPARATE their voices and to recognize how they react in our bodies.

In the final months of my first pastorate in 1996, stress rose to high decibel counts. Nameless fears nagged all day long.

The more I tried to fight the problem, through mindless analyzing, worrying, fretting and projecting, the worse it became. The fruit of my efforts manifested in a stubborn kidney stone, which refused to budge. After nine long months of failed manipulations, the devil-shaped stone was extracted, and with it a lesson!

My kidney stone was self-inflicted!

Worry and fear had upset the delicate chemical balance in my body and had precipitated a clawing monster in my urethra. How I wished I had known what I know now!

There exists an invisible link between festering emotions and thoughts and what goes on in the body.

1. ANCIENT MEDICINE LINKS THE TWO

Chinese medicine understands this connection between emotions, thoughts, and sickness. Dr. Hong Zhen Zhu, who practices in Vancouver, British Columbia, sets out this relationship in his book *Building a Jade Screen*. According to Chinese Medicine, three types of emotional conditions create problems in the body (page 36):

Constantly out of control emotions creating obsessions
Sudden emotional bursts, in anger and fear
Prolonged emotional periods of grief or bitterness

Dr. Zhu writes that men are more likely to internalize their anger than women and to suffer from suppressed emotions. Anger affects the chemical activities in the body, especially the mucous membranes of the stomach. Women have a tendency to become ill from sorrow. Older people are more prone to suffer from sorrow, anxiety, and too much thinking! He connects the sicknesses in our organs to unruly emotions:

-**a**nger affects the liver and stomach
-over-excitement the heart
-sorrow the lungs
-fear and terror the kidneys
-too much thinking the spleen
-greed the heart and mind, making it unstable (ibid, page 37).

2. MEDICAL SCIENCE SEES THE LINK

Excessive anxiety causes more than just an acid stomach or a headache. Western medical science has long since recognized that our body organs are intimately involved with what we do, feel, and think. Our organs store experiences, good and bad, in their memory banks.

In her book, The *Anxiety Epidemic*, Billie Jay Sahley, Ph.D. (Texas: The Pain & Stress Center) believes the gut lining of our stomach, esophagus, small intestine, and the colon not only have brains, but also memory! Now other researchers are saying the same thing.

Dr Michael Gershon, professor of anatomy and cell biology, reported in the New York Times, January 23, 1996, that gastrointestinal disorders, such as colitis, irritable bowel syndrome, diverticulitis, diarrhea, constipation and the like, are linked to prolonged emotional pain and anxiety. Colon irrigation has shown how memories may trigger during the process of purging, creating flashbacks into traumatic experiences in the past. This is because the brain communicates directly with the gut 'brain' by way of chemical messengers or neurotransmitters.

Gabor Mate, M.D., in his article, *The Stress of It All* (*Toronto:* The Globe & Mail, June 22, 2002), observed direct links in patients who had *shut down* emotionally, to degenerative diseases, such as cancer, rheumatoid arthritis, bowel disorders, chronic fatigue syndrome. The brain's emotional centers, he says, are linked to the immune system of the body.

In 2003, the Canadian Institute of Stress conducted a survey of 1,320 randomly selected Canadians to investigate the relationship of stress to minor ailments (The Globe & Mail, Sept. 13, 2003). Among the most common conditions experienced were the following: tooth grinding (19%); insomnia (41%); frequent colds and flu (42%); fatigue (47%); tension headaches (52%); depression and mood swings (56%). Dr. Richard Earle, director of the Institute, states that there *"is still a huge disconnect between what the average person understands about stress and what they are willing to do"* to correct the problem.

In a study undertaken by The Mind/Body Medical Institute at Harvard Medical School, it was found that 60-90% of all visits to the medical office in the United States were emotional and stress related (Medicine in the New Millennium *Daytona Beach News Journal*, January 22, 2000). Suppressing emotions is risky to both physical and mental health.

As Woody Allen once said dryly through one of his characters: *"I never get angry. I grow tumors instead!"*

3. FEAR-FILLED EMOTIONS LINK TO SICKNESS

Fear-filled emotions play key roles in the spread of modern plagues, such as cancer and heart disease.

Gabor Mate (ibid) stated how most cases of breast cancer are linked to hidden mindset roots. One woman's husband, a prominent lawyer and alcoholic, mistreated her. By the time the marriage ended, she was a victim of severe emotional abuse. *"If you ask me why I got cancer, I would tell you it's because I allowed myself to be destroyed in the marriage. I was always afraid of him. I didn't have enough self-respect. I was never good enough for him."* She blamed her disease on buried fears. The cumulative impact of her negativity eventually weakened her immune system.

In the same article, Anna was mentioned as a compulsive caregiver and breast-cancer survivor. She found that deep roots of bitterness and unforgiveness had lodged in her memory as she grew up, *"when early emotional programming and unconscious psychological coping styles accumulated over her lifetime."* Subconsciously, these buried stressors exploded at a time of great trauma, making her vulnerable to a fatal disease.

Dr. Paul Meier recently stated in an interview with Joyce Meyer (CTS, March 15, 2004) that 90% of anxiety-panic disorders have roots in fear-filled emotional pain. The other 10% are genetic.

Janice didn't like the results of her bone density and cholesterol tests. Following an accident, her bones honey-combed to those similar to that of a 75-year-old—and she was only 51! Her cholesterol level had shot up to around 8. The doctor issued a stern warning: *"If the numbers do not come down soon, you'll need a strong prescription to reverse the trend."*

She immediately took responsibility for her own health, entering into a strict regime of raw foods and weekly exercise programs. But after a year, her next test was even worse than the last. She cried out to the Lord for answers. A few days later, the answer came from Henry Wright's book: *"Cholesterol is directly related to people who are very, very angry with themselves. There is a high degree of self-deprecation; they're always putting themselves down"* (ibid, page 130). Pastor Wright also states that osteoporosis has its roots in envy and jealousy (ibid, page 143).

"I took a hard look at myself. It was true! I hated myself. I was always putting myself down in a hostile way. I was full of envy. No wonder my cholesterol was high! As I freed myself of my bitter-root fears, my cholesterol and bone density steadily improved... I now have more peace and don't feel as stressed."

The only difference Janice had made in her daily health routines was a change in the way she thought about herself!

According to Janet Maccaro, thoughts of love cause the body to release interleukin and interferon, which make us feel peaceful and relaxed. Anxious thoughts, on the other hand, release cortisone and adrenaline, which suppress the immune system, and make us susceptible to sickness.

REJECTION LINKS TO DISEASE

Evidence is mounting that many specific sicknesses relate to emotional roots in childhood.

Rejection, for example, is a nagging pain that never leaves. It hides in the subconscious, waiting to move upwards in an emotional burst that confuses the mind. The delicate balance of the body systems is then compromised; the body then weakens under the stress.

Most people prefer to keep their sickness separate from their emotional and mental sicknesses. They dull their pain of rejection by withdrawing in shame, inflicting themselves with drugs, or by aggressive patterns of behavior designed to lift them in pride.

> **Evidence is mounting that many specific sicknesses relate to emotional roots in childhood.**

Rejection and insecurity are modern-day plagues. Hospitals cater to a large group   of people, Christians and non-Christians, who hold unresolved rejection and resentments in their hearts. *"A calm {and} undisturbed mind {and} heart are the life {and} health of the body, but envy, jealousy, {and} wrath are like rottenness of the bones"* (Proverbs 14.30).

Rejection links to fibromyalgia

E.A. Walker, Department of Psychiatry and Behavioral Sciences, University of Washington, tells us that *"sexual, physical and emotional trauma may be important factors in the development and maintenance of fibromyalgia and its associated disability in many patients"* (E-mail letter from Pleasant Valley, November 2004).

In this letter, Pastor Wright discusses this link. Fibromyalgia, he says, is a chronic disorder, characterized by fatigue and muscle pain over 11-18% of the body. The medical community has no cure for fibromyalgia. People with this syndrome may also experience sleep disturbances, irritable bowel syndrome, and other symptoms.

Pastor Wright sees the pain of this disease as psychogenic, or spiritually rooted. The culprit behind this illness is not an infection or inflammation, but a season (or lifetime) of fear, anxiety, and rejection.

According to the Mayo Clinic, (ibid, page 2) *"fibromyalgia affects 3 to 8 million Americans. Approximately 90 percent of those affected are women. The Merck manual pinpoints it further, saying that this disease affects primarily females who are stressed, tense, driven, anxious, and striving* (in their rejection). Spiritually, these unresolved emotional tensions, open wide pathways to serious disease.

When there is abuse in the home, the child feels the pain of rejection deep in his soul. Rejection turns into bitterness and unloving thoughts that play on the child's mind. The child grows up expecting to be rejected again. He feels victimized and unsafe. As a result, the body is kept in a constant state of fight or flight.

The cause of many diseases, such as Fibromyalgia, Lupus, and Parkinson's can be linked to shame and deep feelings of rejection in childhood. When the spiritual cover of the father, for example, is torn away and he leaves, the child suffers rejection by a thousand and one cuts. Fear of being rejected again spreads throughout his body and develops roots for future sicknesses. *"There is no fear in love; but perfect love casts out fear because fear involves torment. But he who fears has not been made perfect in love"* (1 John 4:18, NKJV).

Sid could hardly move. By his late forties, he had developed all the manifestations of fibromyalgia. For days, pain racked his muscles and joints. After becoming a Christian, counseling revealed bitterness in his heart towards his dad. *"I could never get close to my dad. He never believed I could do anything worthwhile. In his eyes I was 'a no good.' I hated him with a passion for what he did to me. I felt abandoned by him."* When he allowed God to take His rightful place in his life, all sense of unworthiness and rejection began to lift. For the first time, he experienced the peace of God within.

Deliverance from inner shame, rejection, and bitterness, restored the spiritual cover over the family, and also his health. Gradually, he was able to withdraw from the heavy medications offered by his doctors for his physical pain. Only as the flames of anger in his heart were doused with the water of the Word did Sid's healing begin. *"When my father and my mother forsake me, then the LORD will take me up"* (Psalms 27:10, KJV). Sid's victory was made complete in Jesus Christ.

Pastor Wright, in his book *A More Excellent Way,* lists numerous connections between sickness and their emotional roots. Not surprisingly, roots of fear-filled rejection and self-hatred, link to diseases of every stripe. Feelings of peace, joy, contentment, and right thinking inhibit disease. This is the essence of the teaching of the Word of God.

The cause of many diseases such as Fibromyalgia, Lupus, and Parkinson's disease can be linked to shame and deep feelings of rejection in childhood.

According to recent experiments by neuroscientists at the University of Montreal, *position emission tomography* has demonstrated a link existing between emotions, thoughts, and serotonin levels. Positive emotional and mental activities are known to activate the frontal lobe of the brain, decreasing anxiety. Serotonin, as a mood regulator, induces contentment. They concluded their study by stating that serotonin levels are controlled by thinking right!

4. SCRIPTURE LINKS THE TWO

As I searched for answers, I began to see how scripture links disease to what we feel and think. It is a recurring theme in the

Word of God, but I had not seen it before!

King Solomon, for example, gave us important verses which were designed to lead us into higher ways of thinking: *"Death and life are in the power of the tongue, and they who indulge in it shall eat the fruit of it (for death or life)"* (Proverbs 18:21).

Righteous thoughts create life: negative thinking results in terminal degenerative diseases, such as cancer. Proverbs even connects lust to pain in the liver: *"Till a dart (of passion) pierces and inflames his vitals* [liver in KJV]... *not knowing that it will cost him his life"* (Proverbs 7:23).

Solomon also tells us that when we think happy thoughts, our thoughts tone up our body: they are as good as medicine. In medical language, they raise serotonin levels. But thoughts emanating from unresolved internal wounds of the soul, such as rejection or bitterness, weaken the bones, lowering serotonin levels: *"A happy heart is good medicine, and a cheerful mind works healing, but a broken spirit dries up the bones"* (Proverbs 17:22). Red corpuscles form in the bone marrow. It is clear from this Word that production of our blood in the bone marrow is highly sensitive to the kinds of emotions and thoughts we allow our minds to process.

Jesus further amplifies this connection. In the story of the paralyzed man who was brought to Jesus, He tied the man's physical and emotional sickness together, first ministering healing to his body. Then Jesus went directly to the heart of the man, when He said: *"your sins are forgiven and the penalty remitted"* (Matthew 9:1-7). He might have said: "It was the sin in your heart that made you sick in the first place. As long as you rejoice in God and are content, your body functions will do their work to keep you well. So in your new walk, don't let your feelings and thinking make you sick again" (my paraphrase).

God does not want us sick, but healthy, and happy! By purging the inner life of all that corrupts, the body is cleansed of its body wastes!

Yet Scripture tells us that God heals us of all our diseases, including emotional problems. *"[He] forgives all your iniquities... heals all your diseases"* (Psalms 103:3 NKJV). We have a better covenant with God. *"Beloved, I pray that you may prosper in all things and be in health, just as your soul prospers"* (3 John 2 NKJV). God's perfect will is that we walk in divine health with all our fears held in check by the Holy Spirit.

Regrettably, few Christians are actually healed at church altars today; Christians are just as sick as non-Christians. Could it be that the Church remains largely passive in its thinking toward the healing promises of God? Those who consider themselves as *"spiritually mature"* fall just as sick as the immature and non-Christian. This should not be. The Church is only now recognizing this vital connection between emotions, thoughts, and sickness. which gives hope that the Church of Jesus Christ will not only soon move in spiritual power, but also in divine health and power.

SEPARATION from emotional and mental chaos is an absolute necessity for walking in Christ's freedom and divine health.

Are you willing to let the Lord invade every part of you—your emotions, mind, will and spirit? He came to save us in each of these areas.

ACTION PLAN FOR RECOVERY

I Principles

Stress is more often the fruit, not the root. We harvest in our body what we have previously sown in our mind. Symptoms of stress are expressed inwardly and outwardly, and often relate to unresolved issues in the soul.

Stress should be viewed as a "friend," informing us of disharmony between the body, soul, and spirit. When we recognize our symptoms, we have the choice, either to ignore them or to deal with them.

When our minds are "stayed" upon Jesus Christ, our soul is *"lifted up,"* it rests, is happy and feels balanced in the Spirit. This is the best antidote to stress there is. It is Christ's gift to us, to help us walk with Him in this fallen, fear-filled world.

II Questions

1. *"If someone suggested to you that your cholesterol and heart problems related to your toxic feelings and thought patterns, you, no doubt, would be upset."*

   Are you willing to explore this possibility? Write out any connections you see between your sicknesses and emotional and mental patterning in your life. Pray over them for wisdom as to how you should deal with them.

2. *"A happy heart is good medicine, and a cheerful mind works healing, but a broken spirit dries up the bones"* (Proverbs 17:22).

   Think of the last time you had a *happy* experience. Write down the feelings you had in a list. Then think of the time when you suffered a period of depression. Write down how you felt in

88

your body and in your emotions. Jot down your thoughts. Meditate on this proverb and see Christ's wisdom in it.

III Prayer

Father, thank You for showing me that my stress symptoms possess roots, which I may axe at the Cross. Forgive me for my blindness; it has kept me from seeing how "connected" I am. You have made me a tri-part being-body, soul and spirit, and I now see how stress affects all three. I am willing now to begin SEPARATING the symptoms of my stress to gain more peace in Christ. Give me the grace, I pray, to walk with You in this journey. I pray this in the name of Jesus Christ. Amen.

Part II

Dealing with Stress at its Roots

CHAPTER SIX

Leveling your emotional swings

*"But now put away and rid yourselves (completely) of all
these things: anger, rage, bad feeling toward others, curses
and slander, and foul-mouthed abuse
and shameful utterances from your lips."*
(Colossians 3:8)

Wꞓe have reached a critical part in this book. We are now moving from managing stress in our body, to dealing with the roots of stress in our emotions and thinking. Jesus is asking this question once again: *Do you want to go on?*

In this section, we will be looking into how we may SEPA-RATE away every stressor from our emotions, thoughts, images, imaginations, and cycles. Only then will we see the roots of our stress.

We will do it with the aid of a powerful weapon, which will help grind these root stressors to a powder. Jesus Christ gave it to us at the Cross—it is called FORGIVENESS. With this power tool, we are able to untangle the binding elements of our soul and cast them from us. It is a perfect, but simple solution to an age-old, vexing problem—how to find peace within.

Key #2 "Forgiveness Therapy" destroys the works of chaos in our souls.

This second Key—THE KEY OF FORGIVENESS—will be used throughout the remaining chapters in our walk into freedom. Forgiveness and its twin, repentance, unlock the door to Christ's peace. Forgiveness comes first after the sin has been recognized. Then we turn away from the sin. Forgiveness is a platform from which the Holy Spirit is able to work, releasing the souls of God's people from bondage into Christ's liberty and peace.

The statement *"Lord Jesus, please forgive me"* swings Heaven's door wide open by faith. Jesus then flows back to us His assurance with peace, to indicate our forgiveness has been received. This kind of forgiveness may only be received from one person— Jesus Christ, the High Priest of Heaven.

> **Unforgiveness is the devil's *soma* pill. It numbs out the *will* of God's people.**

APPLYING FORGIVENESS AS THERAPY

Forgiveness is not a one-time event, completed when we were born anew at the altar. For all those who love the Lord Jesus Christ, forgiveness is a practical lifestyle. When the balm of forgiveness is applied every day, the soul releases its toxic build-ups. Breaking the power of *S.I.S* is really a leap into this freeing lifestyle. With its daily application, it changes us into Christ's image.

Walking in forgiveness keeps us humble and tender before the Lord.

Unforgiveness is the devil's *soma* pill. It numbs out the *will* of God's people. The devil's aim is to disable every individual's ability to choose for God. If he can get us to believe forgiveness is no longer necessary—that it was all taken care of at the Cross—the pill has worked. If he can get us to believe our bitter feelings are not rooted in unforgiveness, and are irrelevant to our walk with Jesus, then he has successfully dulled our minds into passivity. His poison continues to flow in us unnoticed, whether in an individual or a Church group.

Unforgiveness hardens the soul. It is an unloving spirit that freely transfers itself between saints, defiling many in the process. When unforgiveness is allowed to remain, spiritual potential becomes restricted.

Every Christian must learn to hate the devil's works (1 John 3:8). Jesus warns us, that in our world, offences will come. When they do, we must be quick to apply the balm of forgiveness, as soon as any hurt rises in our hearts, to neutralize the devil's soma. The helmet of salvation must be on tight each day! Bitterness and unforgiveness are chain links the devil employs to pull us down into pits of stress and sickness. If you say you have forgiven someone, but the emotional pain still throbs within, then the balm needs to be applied until you sense Christ's peace over the hurt.

To forgive is not an option; it is a command of God. If the Church of Jesus Christ is to know power, every unforgiving spirit must be brought into the Light of the Holy Spirit. Only then will individuals in the Church be able to fully bear the waves of His coming glory.

The Spirit of Forgiveness is a cleansing agent, which is a prime requirement in forming a glorious Bride for Jesus Christ! Even now, the Holy Spirit is applying this balm to millions in the present day harvesting of souls around the world.

Below is the scripture most often used to bring us into FORGIVENESS:

"If we confess our sins, He is faithful and just to forgive us our sins and to cleanse us from all unrighteousness" (1 John 1:9, KJV).

What do we confess and ask forgiveness for? We ask forgiveness for worrying and being anxious. We bring before Him the bitter judgments we have made against others and for allowing expressions of fear, shame, guilt, and pride to hinder our walk with Jesus, which shuts out the grace of God. We ask forgiveness for allowing our toxic thinking to bind our past to our future, preventing God's intervention in our lives.

When we forgive others, God, and ourselves like this, we sense the heartbeat of Jesus. Forgiveness applied correctly always brings us into the rest of God.

My first task was to find and SEPARATE every unruly emotion and its root. They needed to be exposed in the Light of the Holy Spirit. First, I had to own them, and take responsibility for them.

WHAT ARE EMOTIONS?

Webster's Dictionary tells us an *"emotion"* is any strong agitation of feelings, usually accompanied by physiological changes. Emotional decisions are usually wrong, it says. A root of the word also describes emotions as *"moving away."* Agitated feelings, anger, hate, even over excitement, move us away from the centre of calm. They lead us into imbalance and stress, and away from God.

1. Emotions are a God-given, internal thermometer

Emotions are a register that respond to whatever we think and sense in our bodies. They run hot or cold, positive and negative in us, providing a reliable measure of our stability and maturity. We will always have emotions. It is what we do with them that count. We may use them for either good or evil; the choice is always ours. But so often, we are passively involved and tend to ignore our God-given right to control them under the power of the Holy Spirit.

Jesus was always in control of His emotions (Hebrews 13:8). So should we! Through them, we are able to enjoy life and to endure in His Grace. Every intense moment is remembered through our emotions. If our emotions do not kick in watching a sunset, it passes by unnoticed.

2. Emotions cradle messages

Emotions welling up in us should cause us to ask questions: What am I feeling? What do they say? Have I ever felt like this before? Emotions transport vital messages, both positive and negative. Most of us don't ever think of emotions this way. Being passionate about your golf game means that your feelings empower your thoughts about the game—they go together: they both help you to focus on the ball. Emotions weld to thoughts like two sides of a coin. But there are other emotions that cradle messages that run in our subconscious mind—we don't know they are there!

If we desire to live stable, disciplined lives in the Spirit, we need not only to be in touch with our feelings; we need also to SEPARATE them out in order to find what they say. In general, positive emotions lead us to God; negative emotions lead us away from God.

> ## Positive emotions lead us to God; negative emotions lead us away from God.

3. Emotions are volatile

Volatile emotions belong to the bitter or traumatized individual, while stable, gently rolling emotions, under the control of the Holy Spirit, belong to those with spiritual strength.

David's question about the condition of his soul clued me in on the behavior of emotions. In Psalms 42:11, he asked: *"Why are you cast down, O my inner self?"* Implicit in his words is the idea that the soul and spirit contract or expand within us. Shame-based emotions tend to pull down the soul: we feel depressed, lonely, and guilty in our sink-holes. On the other hand, pride tends to puff the soul, making us feel special, and proud of our abilities. We feel we are "number one."

Emotions are always on the move. They are never still. In one moment, they sink in shame and despair, and in the next rise in pride-filled confidence. This is a trick of self, to keep us off balance.

I had always thought the violent swings of my emotions were just me! They were who I was—the result of being human. But their ups and downs created a fall-out in confusion, insecurity, and great difficulty in relating to others. Emotional volatility was the pattern of my life, all through my school years. I was controlled by them. As a result, I failed in every subject, except art. I read my first book at the age of sixteen, which took six months to finish! My headmaster gracelessly discussed my school record before my shocked parents: *"He will always have to work with his hands,"* he said, meaning that whatever latent brain power God had given me, it had been confined to my thumbs!

At twenty-one, I returned to basic education classes, with my peers already embarking upon their professional careers. I graduated from University with two degrees, with more than a third of my life over—at twenty-nine! The devil had robbed me of many years. I have asked God to compensate for those lost years, by adding them to the end of my allotted three score and ten. That would bring me at least to 100!

Even after graduation from University, I still suffered these wild swinging emotions, without ever wondering at their cause. For my first job, I told my mother I was off to Borneo: *"It's at the end of the world! I might find myself out there."* I didn't know who I was! Insecurity had wormed through my personality. Getting alone with myself, isolated in those primeval forests, far from people, might give me answers. Looking back, I realize my emotional state was aptly described in Scripture: *"He who has no rule over his own spirit is like a city that is broken down and without walls"* (Proverbs 25:28).

4. Emotions can be suppressed, but at a cost

Pushing down emotions, or trying to cap them, is a costly practice. They will find expression somehow, even if it is through the body in sickness. Failing to deal with anxiety, rage, and anger, as they occur, may stunt emotional development for years. I never thought much about my own strong feelings simmering deep within me: they were never important enough to consider, no matter how many times they exploded. The reason: their contained thoughts had been so completely buried I never knew they were there! This is how Satan conquers our will; by rending our emotions and thinking passive toward God.

As an Englishman, I was all too familiar with the popular mantra of our society: *"Keep a stiff upper lip,"* which means—*"no emotions in public, please! Bottle them! Ignore them. Don't ever express them!"* Feelings were not something you talked about. Hiding them behind an inner iron wall of my thinking became a convenient protective device to keep me from being hurt again, but sometimes it didn't work!

In refusing to see these occasional emotional bursts as message carriers, I postponed my healing. Psalm 32:6 explained this for me: *"For this (forgiveness) let everyone who is godly pray—pray to You in a time when You may be found."* As a result, I put-off God's appointed times for the Holy Spirit to start His work in me for many years. I had declared feelings irrelevant. They were of little use in carving a career, so why bother with them?

Pushing down emotions, or trying to cap them, is a costly practice. Failing to deal with anxiety, rage, and anger, as they occur, may stunt emotional development for years.

Stuffing them down means we don't know what to do with them. We never ask questions: Why are they there? What are they trying to show me? We need to step back and look objectively at them. We need to understand them, letting them be our friends and not our enemies.

Dr. Ed Smith was the first to describe how buried wounds give off their own peculiar *"smoke,"* signaling that something is wrong below (Psalm 68:1-2). This subterranean smoldering was a part of my emotional life! I just went along with it. With amazing regularity, this volcanic steam would blow, leaving me confused and feeling ill, wondering *"where did that come from?"*

Married life is one of the best arenas to understand feelings. I not only had to learn the language of this vague, transitory world, but to use feelings as a subject in everyday conversation. It was not an easy process. I had to climb over my walls to find them. As I began to name them, and observe them, I began to understand their role.

5. *Emotions develop spiral traps*

We rarely ever consider our negative emotions as part of a programmed downward spiral, inspired of Satan. His strategy is to pull us into his D's—disappointment, discouragement, defeat, and despair, linking one dark emotion to another, moving us always downward.

Isolated emotions rise and fall as they may, but if left alone, they lock into other more damaging emotions and pull us into an out-of-control emotional vortex. The deeper we fall into this maelstrom of feelings, the darker and more stressful it becomes. Sin adds to sin and stress also adds to more stress!

In their landmark Prayer Counseling Course, John and Paula Sandford emphasized that every negative emotion should be examined and SEPARATED out as they arise.

If we fail to see this interlocking feature of our emotions, we may pay a high price for ignorance and passivity.

This was something I had never done. When one bold prayer warrior in our group suggested I harbored "rage" deep down, I was mortified! I thought her elevator had stuck between floors.

"Impossible," I blustered within. I had never ever displayed raw emotions like this one! Ask my wife! Soon after, the truth dawned that my rage was a part of a repressed memory in my childhood. I had capped it with a vow: *"I will never show feelings to anyone— ever again."* Since childhood, I had lived in denial of my own emotional makeup. An inner refusal stopped me from registering their moments, when they flew upwards.

SLIDE OF STRESSOR EMOTIONS

(Pain of a hurt starts the slide in worry)

EMOTION	REASON
Worry and anxiety	Looking into the future
Fear	Expecting it will happen again
Bitterness	Judgements interpreting the hurt
Anger	Bitterness expresses itself
Unforgiveness	Keeps mental record of offences
Resentment	Feelings of ill will toward others
Depression	Hurt will never be resolved
Despair	There is no longer any hope
Suicide	Fascination with death

Or

Retaliation	Desire to get even
Violence	Outwardly expressing hatred
Murder	Desire to even the score

Figure 4. The slide of stressor emotions

Note that fear wraps every emotion. Each new emotional level demands more energy to control its unruliness. Every born-again believer should make it a priority to understand these fear-filled, soulish emotions and their path down into a vortex managed by the devil. If we fail to see this interlocking feature of our emotions, we may pay a high price for ignorance and passivity.

Each emotion on the slide is a stressor. Each must be exposed to the Light of the Holy Spirit. Our heavenly Father is developing a

Bride, glorious, without spot, or wrinkle, free from every one of these dead-weight emotions.

Whenever you feel like you're being sucked into this spiral, you should immediately pause and ask yourself some questions: *"Is the Lord trying to get me to bring my feelings before Him? Whom do I need to forgive? Are my feelings self-inflicted'?*

A quiet, unruffled spirit within is the measure of Christ we all long for. FORGIVENESS is the Key that releases Christ's peace within us. It lays the foundation soil for the impartation of His creative seeds. If we neglect this vital key applied to our emotions we may easily miss His best for us.

WORRY STARTS THE SLIDE

Crises often drag us into emotional spirals. A hurtful remark, a wrong decision, or loss is enough to trigger worry and anxiety feelings. Worry is simply pride trying to work things out! But beneath the pride, run deep fears of being exposed and shamed; there is a fear of failing and of being rejected again.

Although Jesus sternly warned us not to worry or be anxious, most Christians still do! The Body of Christ needs the revelation in our hearts that the spirit of mammon is no longer taking care of us —Jesus is now in charge! Worry is the first emotion to separate us from tomorrow's victory.

If we fail to check worry at the gate of our mind, our thinking descends into waywardness. We become judgmental, bitter, and angry, which opens the mouth of the spiral. This is why Jesus had so much to say about worry in Matthew 6. Worry and anxiety sit on top of the emotional funnel. If we fail to switch off the currents of worry and anxiety, inevitably they will drag us into the abyss.

Worry then, has its primary root in shame. To cope, we try to work out our problems, fearing more failure and shame, each time falling short before God and man.

Worry then, has its primary root in shame. To cope, we try to work out our problems,

fearing more failure and shame, each time falling short before God and man.

Worry is a dead emotion, but carries with it subtle deceptions. As a long-time worry addict, I had even bought the deception that *"worry helps me to think and to solve my problems. If I worry long and hard enough, I will make my own future."* Self was firmly in command, as a fiery, petulant boss ruling from his throne. *"And who of you by worrying and being anxious can add one unit of measure (cubit) to his stature or to the span of his life?"* (Matthew 6:27).

Worry hooks us into the world, the flesh, and the devil, cultivating obsessive ties to the cares of life. It is a pain that carries an insatiable lust for satisfaction, which never comes. This is why worry is as addictive as cocaine. It leads the pack into the pit.

To find the source of my own chronic worrying and anxieties, I revisited my early years with counselors. I was shocked to find that my childhood was far from normal. In today's language, I would have been labeled as having a *"severe detachment syndrome"* with *"sociophobic tendencies."* Worry and fear of being rejected again held me captive in shame. This was the root that needed to be exposed. The more I applied the Key of FORGIVENESS, the more I was able to overcome worry's prodding menace.

Dora's response to her sister-in-law's interference in a private matter was out of all proportion to the incident. Her emotional outburst was a sure sign of earlier wounding. She felt herself being sucked down into a pit of blackness. *"So much pain left me trembling. Numbness crept over me. I seemed to be worrying and fearful about something I couldn't name. Alone in my car afterwards, I sensed something had gone horribly wrong but couldn't define it. I felt violated and then anger began to roll over me."*

Counseling revealed similar emotional blow-ups had occurred many times in Dora's life. The pattern was always about the same. But she never understood why her feelings occasionally boiled out of control. When we looked into her childhood, we found the root cause. Her mom had berated her incessantly with harsh put-downs. *"Each time, the hate for my mom grew. She was destroying me. I walked around for days numbed out, a horrible blackness over me. As I grew older, I tried to cope with these rampaging feelings by stuffing them down. It didn't work too well."*

Whenever Dora was at the wrong end of a confrontation, her unhealed childhood memories sent a familiar *expectation* into her conscious mind: *"They are out to destroy me!"* Worry and fear of rejection triggered the anger and bitterness in her and the spiral downward took hold. Without realizing it, her sister-in-law had become her mom. Dora saw the connection and the thoughts that had impaled her life. As she applied the Key of FORGIVENESS to her mom and to herself, the power of her expectations broke and the deep bitterness lifted from her. She was at last set free. The tensions in her soul began to ease; her thinking cleared, and her speech tones relaxed. Her mind came to rest in Jesus.

HANDLING EMOTIONS CORRECTLY

Jesus lived in a stressful time, just as we do. So how did Jesus handle His anxious moments? He simply lifted them up to His Father in Heaven, and He left them there. He stayed in His Father's peace.

Many times Jesus displayed His feelings openly in public, but never lost control! Over Jerusalem *"He wept."* In the Garden of Gethsemane, He suffered greatly: *"My soul is exceeding sorrowful!"* (Matthew 26:38, KJV); *"Now is my soul troubled"* (John 12:27 KJV). Jesus never denied his emotions, nor did He ever ignore them or push them down.

That Jesus had perfect control over His emotions is best seen during the darkest periods of His earthly ministry. Throughout His trial, and on way to the Cross, not once do we see Jesus ever stepping into His flesh, bowing to the dictates of His *self* nature. He refused to indulge in the prideful ways of the carnal, hurling bitter, critical judgments at His captives. *"When He was reviled and insulted, He did not revile or offer insult in return..."* (1 Peter 2:23). This statement speaks of the discipline Jesus exercised over His emotions and words. (Jesus reserved His acid judgments for those who should have known better—the Pharisees.)

Nor do we see any expressions of shame and self-pity during His trial. Rather, Jesus fully owned, identified, and was responsible at all times for His feelings. When His disciples and followers abandoned Him, He saw it as a part of His prophetically inspired mission. He never allowed His feelings to descend into an emotional spiral. Instead, He blessed all around Him with His FORGIVENESS. This is how we should be. Jesus' way should be our way.

Jesus tells us that the primary positive emotion given to all saints at their new birth is Christ's peace: *"Peace I leave with you; My {own} peace I now give and bequeath to you"* (John 14:27). I knew that if I could control my emotions, I could change my behavior. I made it my number one goal, to protect Christ's peace within me.

Not once do we see Jesus ever stepping into His flesh, bowing to the dictates of His self nature.

How did Paul handle his emotions? The Apostle Paul also took full responsibility for his emotions. That he guarded the precious gift of peace Christ had given him, is seen in his own words: God *"has called us to peace* (1 Corinthians 7:15); we are to *"strive to live in peace* (Hebrews 12:14) and to*" preach the gospel of peace"* (Romans 10:15 KJV). Yet, even Paul handled this treasure carelessly—once!

Paul, a prisoner in the Caesarea Court of Justice, was ordered to be struck by the guards. Instead of submitting, Paul lashed out in anger: *"God* is *about to strike you, you whitewashed wall!"* (Acts 23:3). Paul was told that his reference to whitewashing a pigpen was an insult! He had unknowingly hurled it at the High Priest! He saw his mistake and made a choice. He could admit he had broken a Law of God (Exodus 22:28) before the court and repent; or stay in his anger. Paul chose the former and asked for forgiveness for his rash act.

This is how we should handle our emotions. Allow your feelings to rise in order to SEPARATE them. Then name them. If there is bitterness or anger, there must be a decision to walk out of the pain through the door of FORGIVENESS. Our heavenly Father will give His assurance of peace that He has heard you. He loves you as you are, even in your pain, but loves you too much to leave you there.

Are you willing to give the Lord your toxic emotions each day? He is ready and willing to lift off your pain and give you His peace.

ACTION PLAN FOR RECOVERY

I Principles

1. FORGIVENESS is the Key that unlocks the door to Christ's peace. By using this Key, we release ourselves from the stress we create through our ungodly emotional patterning.

2. Emotions either give life or inflict stress. We must cooperate with the Holy Spirit to deal with them if we are to know peace in Christ.

3. Emotions rarely act alone; they like company! They will join with others if we passively allow them to rule. If unruly emotions are not stopped by using the Key of FORGIVE-NESS, they will pull us down into greater levels of stress.

4. Buried wounds in the soul, especially those inflicted during childhood, give off emotional *smoke signals,* to tell us that something is wrong—that a wound needs healing (Psalm 68:1-2).

II Questions

1. *"Unforgiveness is the devil's soma pill. It numbs out the will of God's people."*

When you first came to the Lord, were you taught that forgiveness was an event, or a lifestyle? After reading this chapter, do you see the importance of living each day in FORGIVENESS? If there is bitterness and hurt still lodged in your heart, I suggest that you go back through your life and write down everyone who hurt you. Don't forget to write down those you hurt by your words and actions. Then choose to use this Key, until there is absolutely no more pain. (Remember, you may have carried the hurt for a long time, so the process of healing may also take time).

2. *"Emotions operate as a thermometer, providing us with a reliable measure of our stability and maturity."*

Do you find that your emotions swing wildly for no reason? Try plotting them during the course of a week. Name them. Ask the Holy Spirit to help you find the root judgments made in bitterness. Then begin to level them through FORGIVENESS.

3. Read Matthew 26:36-46. Make a list of all the emotions that Jesus experienced in the Garden of Gethsemane. What did Jesus do with His feelings? Do you see this as an example of how we are to deal with our own negative emotions?

III Prayer

Father, I realize I have allowed my emotions to come and go as they please. I have listened more to them than to You! I've often allowed myself to be led by them. Please forgive me. I see now that the best antidote to stress is this Key of FORGIVENESS. It is the way into Your peace. Help me to bring my worries and anxieties to You and to use the Key of FORGIVENESS to level my emotions. Lord, I choose to forgive _____ for hurting me. I have held bitterness, anger, and resentment in my heart toward _____. Thank You, Lord Jesus for giving me Your peace and showing me Your way. Amen.

CHAPTER SEVEN

Breaking your box thinking

"When I was a child, I talked like a child, I thought like a child, I reasoned like a child; now that I have become a man, I am done with childish ways and have put them aside."
(1 Corinthians 13:11)

GOD GAVE US A MIND TO CAPTURE HIS!

God gave us a unique ability to think, for the purpose of communing and fellowshipping with Him. *"Come now, and let us reason together, says the Lord"* (Isaiah 1:18). Our brains were designed as stations with antennas to receive a steady flow of thoughts from God. Our responsibility is to mull them over, reason with them, speak them out, and then to act upon them.

"Give us our daily bread" (Matthew 6:11) means we Covenant with God to receive our daily portion of thoughts, wisdom, and guidance from the Lord Jesus Christ, who is the Bread of Life (John 6:35). We then are able to bless our families, and others and ourselves with the goods of this world. *"Man does not live by bread only, but man lives by every word that proceeds out of the mouth of the Lord"* (Deuteronomy 8:3b).

Thoughts are the basic unit of the mind. A single thought not only has spiritual weight, but power, which can influence our behavior and others far into the future. Thoughts move on micromilli-volts of life energy, flowing through the brain in nanoseconds. Hundreds of isolated thoughts pass through our minds each day, all competing for attention and supremacy. Most come from the world, the flesh, and the devil. Sadly, in our fallen-ness, we catch only a few from God!

Webster's Dictionary tells us that a single thought is an idea or notion. We collect these notions into patterns, which help define who we are: *"For as he* [man] *thinks in his heart, so is he"* (Proverbs 23:7, NKJV). Thinking in patterns is an easy way to deal with ourselves, and with others. They help to express ourselves quickly and without effort. It is nature's way of saving time and energy; we then can be occupied with more creative thinking. When our thoughts are fixed upon God, we live in peace (Isaiah 26:3; Philippians 4:7). When they are not, we live in stress!

David allowed God's thoughts to flow freely through him: *"How precious and weighty also are Your thoughts to me, O God! How vast is the sum of them!"* (Psalms 139:17) God's words ensured David's success: *"He will cause your thoughts to become agreeable to His will, and so shall your plans be established and succeed"* (Proverbs 16:3).

SATAN WANTS YOUR MIND!

In his hate-filled opposition to God, Satan has launched an all out offensive to capture every mind. He wants total control. If he can make us slaves to his will, he will. He plays his war games well and with deadly skill, stealing our peace in his attempts to utterly destroy our minds.

I saw how necessary it was to understand the strategies the devil employs to snare our minds. This was a vital step in the SEPARA-TION process. Below are some of the strategies I discovered in my journey walking out of stress:

1. He tempts us to agree with him

His strategy is simple: Satan, as the *"father"* of lies (John 8:44), has only one weapon—deception! He weaves his lies into accusations and hurls them, as fiery darts, into our minds. He knows our weaknesses and plays into them. When he shouts into our ear *"You are a failure,"* our tendency is to agree in worry and fear without hesitation!

We are even tempted to play with his accusations and suggestions in our minds and even add our own negative mindsets to his. If we surrender our mind to him, we will gradually come to think like he does. His purpose is to make us his prisoners behind steel bars forged by our own thinking.

If he can deceive us into thinking his thoughts are ours, he can invade our minds whenever he wants to. So long as he remains hidden and invisible, his work goes unchallenged. We don't realize who is speaking! Agreeing with the devil's suggestions are our wages for serving him. But the end is always the same—sin, stress, sickness, and death.

2. He entices us to think negatively

No one can afford the expense of negative thinking. It is costly and addictive. It is also sin!

Satan wants us to think his way—negatively and destructively, but his way cheapens life, dragging us low into carnal living, and separating us from God. A *"negative thinker"* sends signals that his soul is unwell. This kind of thinker finds something wrong with everything and everyone. Our minds are marvelous instruments given by God, but they make a poor master when they are wrongly used.

No one can afford the expense of negative thinking. It is costly and addictive. It is also sin!

Most of us grow up thinking this way. I certainly did! Here are some typical negative thoughts that floated often across my mind, all of which prompted worry and anxiety to escalate. Circle those you often use. Be honest!

"I'm no good"
"I can't cope"
"I can't do anything right"
"I belong in the background"
"I am afraid to be noticed"
"It's their fault"
"I'll show them"
"No one will tell me what to do"
"I can do better than they can"
"I'm going to be boss"
"I must look after myself"

Every unrenewed mind is familiar with these negative exclamations. I knew that if I were to enter the rest of God (Hebrews 4:11), every ungodly thought would have to be SEPARATED and cast out of my mind.

Tammy, a friend of ours, was given a revelation of how to deal with her negative mind. The Lord compared her negative thoughts to *wily, cunning foxes.* She understood the Lord to say it this way: *"These pesky animals dart across the front of your mind, chasing each other's tails! They move in packs, hiding along the way, making it hard for you to see them. But once you recognize them, just reach up, snatch them from your mind and break their backs!"*

Foxes run in the darkness of our subconscious. By asking the Holy Spirit to shine His light upon them, you will see them.

There is a powerful principle here. These *foxes* are **lies** of the devil. They run in the darkness of our subconscious. By asking the Holy Spirit to shine His light upon them, you will see them. It is easier, then, to grab them and break their backs. Remember, God will not do it for you. It is our responsibility to clean up our attic! In our ignorance, we befriend these foxes in our minds: we even entertain them! Now and then they throw a party—running around so fast, they create whirlwinds of confusion, worry, and anxiety (Psalms 37: 1).

Had I been aware of this principle I would have saved myself from much grief. These lying foxes had established fixed routes in my mind, making me *"feel"* stressed and unable to access the thoughts of God. This is why my stressed out mind, at times, had become a chaotic wasteland. I could only *feel* my stress, not understand it. Had I understood this, I could have laid traps for these urchins of the darkness and barred access to their race tracks cutting my mind.

Rick was five, when his aunt insensitively aimed a cruel word into his impressionable mind: *"You are so ugly!"* she said, delivering a lethal punch to his soul. He believed those idle words and from that moment on, his spirit gradually turned away from people and from life. His mind was bombarded every day with shamed-based thoughts of rejection: *"I am ugly; a misfit. No one wants me, not even God."*

His school years were harrowing. As a teen, he was extremely introverted and rebellious. Cold, panicky fear overwhelmed him whenever he was asked to stand in front of the class to speak. *"By the time I had reached twelve, I was smoking and drinking heavily. There was no relief from the pain deep in my heart."* In his anguish, Rick could only feel the hurt of the rejection; the thought had buried itself in his subconscious mind to continue its iniquitous work in secret.

Later, he developed chronic sociophobia, which yielded only slightly after he became a Christian. He would seat himself on the back row of the church and skip out before the service ended. People terrified him! His anxiety and habitual sense of panicking had developed from one single thought!

Most of us have experienced similar barbed put-downs in childhood. Whether in the home, or in school, careless remarks like these cut deep into a child's spirit. Many flow off us, but others stick like needles. Growing up, I had my share. They were flaming arrows, which ignited fires of negativity in my impressionable mind. I entered adulthood never once questioning why they were there.

One American psychologist, Dr. Martin Seligman, in describing the negative way our society looks at the world and ourselves, tells us in his book *Authentic Happiness* that *"pessimism is fashionable."* Tackling the cause of negative thinking in society, and changing the way people think, he says, would *"require a Titanic turning exercise."* Negative thinking is deeply rooted, and the source of most society ills, including stress.

3. *He turns us into robot thinkers*

Satan tries to numb out our ability to think. His strategy is to build little robots in our minds! In the first Star Wars movie, the lovable robot R2D2 was driven by his internal video-cassette system. No matter the need in the galaxy, this hapless little fellow could do nothing but listen to pre-recorded responses, issued from his built-in recorder system, all played in 3D and color. Robots save us time, but they can create havoc.

The devil seeks to make us all like R2D2! We allow ourselves to be pre-programmed through predictable thought patterns. They provide automatic instructions: what to say; what to feel; and what to do in emotional crises. A robot simply pops a tape! Our responses are then tailor-made. A complete set of emotions is packaged for every occasion, complete with graceless thoughts, expectations, vows, and even smells!

Robots can't tell the difference between yesterday and today, nor can they distinguish between actual circumstances and those imagined. They operate automatically on triggers, popping their nuisance tapes at the most inconvenient times! A single rude or critical remark aimed at you is all it takes for the voluble little robot to spew its ready made pills of condemnation and bitterness into your mind and out of your mouth. Robot thinking chokes off access to God and to others. God is unable to bless you with His thoughts.

4. He causes our minds to race

C.S. Lewis, in his book *Mansoul* illustrates an important principle relating to the mind of man. Man's soul has five gates: the eyes, ears, nose, tongue, and hands. These are the entry points God designed for us to receive His blessings. The devil seeks to clog these gates with his lies and sin-drenched thinking.

Through advertising, cable TV, videos, CD's, DVD's, billboards, internet, Nintendo, e-mails, storms of flashing thoughts and images bombard us daily. They numb the mind and weaken the will. Some stimulate the production of powerful brain chemicals, which, even years afterwards, flashback pictures in the mind. Satan's strategy is to fill our minds with negative thought-images from the world, the flesh and himself. Gradually, the channels of life corrode and become useless (Proverbs 16:22).

The mind of man was never designed for this kind of unrelenting bombardment. Since 1980, Attention Deficit Disorder has become an epidemic among our children and teens. Medical science has no answers. ADD is used to justify the drugging of millions in our schools, when one culprit—TV—sits as an idol in our living rooms. The mind cannot cope with the flashing of these images every split second. It starts to shut down, or race. When we sit in front of the TV or video game for hours, not only the five gates of our senses are open, but the soul opens wide to demonic influence. Serotonin levels are known to plunge. The child's mind hears a cacophony of meaningless sounds, sentences, isolated words, and half-truths. Prescription drugs are then offered to slow down the mind!

Interestingly, in strict homes of the Amish, ADD is unknown. Their slower lifestyles are in harmony with the speed of their brains. Their minds are more at rest, and attention spans are unaffected by this bothersome noise emanating from the high-tech world.

5. He entices us to gaze into the future

Had my conversation with my nurse gone on longer, she might have said *"Don't you see—-it's all in your expectations!"*

John Maxwell says as much: *"Negative expectations are a quick route to a dead end."* They bind us with tight ropes. They choke off creative thinking, and the devil loves it. He would—he inspires them! When we *expect* in a negative way like this, we create pictures in our mind of what is to come. Self tries to control the future—it wants to rule from a high throne!

We think that knowing what lies ahead gives us security. But when *self* tries to see what's coming, we move into forbidden territories belonging to the cults. God alone controls history: He informs whomever He wills. When we worry, we move from the grace of His peace into stress.

I discovered that a large part of my thinking was threaded with *negative expectations,* wrapped in fear. Worry is always a fruit of this straining out of *tomorrow,* seeking for answers that are not there. In a crisis, like Job, I would fear the worst and it often arrived.

Everywhere I voiced my black views. One fund manager from a well-known New York financial institution patiently listened to my descriptions of dark clouds on the world's economic horizon. Bluntly he reprimanded me: *"Listening to you, you'd think the sun won't rise tomorrow!"* He wasn't a Christian—I was!

If God were to take me to higher levels in Him, I knew that every negative expectation, every lie and self-judgment would have to be destroyed, but I had no idea how to do it.

Have you ever spoken fallen, lazy statements like these?

"They will find out who I am."

"I can't do anything right."
"Everything I do end in failure."
"I'm sure to mess up."
"They'll reject me when they find out the real me."
"You can be sure it will turn out bad for me."
"Everything I touch falls apart."
"I will end up embarrassed and feeling stupid."

Of course you have! We all have and, at times, still do. But it is wrong! They all belong to our robot thinking, and we need to see the practice as sin. The Lord is not showing you these things to make you feel guilty; but rather to give you an opportunity to change.

God forbids divining our own future and we are not to compete with Him in the making of it. However, we are tempted constantly to take the reins of the future out of God's hands and put them into ours. God calls us to live one day at a time (Matthew 6:25-32), to be led by His Spirit, not by our own wish list.

God forbids divining our own future and we are not to compete with Him in the making of it.

I was addicted to this type of thinking. It was like a game I played, shuffling my projections on a chessboard. If I thought the worst, and they came true, then I wasn't disappointed. I could even be proud that my forecast was right! If they didn't come to pass, I could thank God they didn't.

The good news is that we don't need to divine the future. God will tell us what we need to know, whenever we need it. He wants our trust to be in Him. It came as a revelation that I don't need to know what is ahead. *"Sufficient for each day is its own trouble"* (Matthew 6:34b).

Remember Rick, whose life was devastated by a cruel remark from his aunt? His healing came when he submitted to counseling.

We traced back the dominant thoughts of his mind to his early child-hood, and found the wound still alive after all these years, complete with crudely fashioned expectations hammering in his subconscious mind. They had pinned him to a future that had no hope.

When the ungracious remark of his aunt was brought into the light, Rick's healing began. He at last saw it as a lie! As he SEPARATED out his toxic emotions and expectations, he was able to bring them before the Lord in FORGIVE-NESS. He forgave his aunt and himself, and released the lie that had bound him: *"I am ugly, no one wants me."* The binding curse over his life broke away. The raw wound in his soul healed.

The next day, Rick went to a special meeting at his church. He strode into the crowded hall and sat himself on the front row. His sociophobic fear had gone! After more than fifty years of carrying pain in his soul, he was finally free! He no longer thought of himself as ugly and with no purpose. The Lord whispered to him: *"You are beautiful in my sight!"* Rick had a new tape to play in his mind. He had heard the truth. It was now up to him to press the button every day and listen.

This is the power behind renewal of the mind! Change comes only when we change our thinking! The power of FORGIVENESS released Rick to walk out of his life-long bondage. Had he contin-ued in unforgiveness, he would have remained chained to the past, unable to free himself from the pain and the continual fear of tomorrow. Only Christ's truth can set us free from this kind of iniq-uitous thinking (Titus 2:14). Jesus went to the Cross to provide us all with an opportunity to change the way we think, to be free in our minds (Isaiah 53:5)!

The Lord wants to renew our thinking, but most of us are not even aware of the thought patterns that govern the running of our lives. We think mostly by habit and our thoughts are buried in our emotions. This is why we need the revelation that every thought must be SEPARATED, and those opposing God brought before

Him in FORGIVENESS and repentance.

My thoughts were so buried in my emotions that I couldn't identify them. This is why the Lord led me first to SEPARATE my emotions, so that my hidden negative thinking could surface and be changed. It was my responsibility to undertake the task, not God's.

HOW TO RENEW YOUR MIND

As I studied the Word, I began to see the contrast between my thinking and the way Jesus thought. My thought patterns were those of the unredeemed. They were squeezed into a tight box, in which there was little or no light. I had conformed my thinking to this world, and adapted it to its external, superficial beliefs (Romans 12:2). If I were to be holy, as God intended, then I had to *let* the Holy Spirit deal with the way I used my mind.

The Apostle Paul grasped this insidious tendency of the mind to slip into worry and anxiety, when he set down the principles of a workable antidote for us in Philippians 4:6-8:

1. Declare your mind a "free-zone" (vs. 6)

"Do not fret or have any anxiety about anything, but in every circumstance and in everything, by prayer and petition (definite requests), with thanksgiving, continue to make your wants known to God."

It is time to claim back your mind for God. Decide for a **Free-Zone**, which bans every type of negative thought. Start with five minutes a day; extend it one hour, then one day. Soon your mind will be under the new management of the Spirit of God

Claim back your mind for God. Decide for a Free-Zone, which bans every type of negative thought.

A good practice is to see your mind as a head of hair! Just as we brush and comb our hair each morning, so we should our minds! Wrong thinking builds tight knots that are hard to dislodge. A good Holy Ghost brush-down will quickly align your thinking to God's way of thinking! Clear your mind of 'dead hair' and debris every morning and sense Christ's peace as you do.

Take responsibility for what goes into your mind and what comes out of it. God waits only for us to begin. John 1:12 says: *"But to as many as did receive {and} welcome Him, He gave the authority (power, privilege, right) to become the children of God, that is, to those who believe in (adhere to, trust in, and rely on) His name...."* Accept responsibility for your own change. Self has inflicted the soul; you must clean it up!

2. Make Christ's peace your goal (vs. 7)

> *"And God's peace [shall be yours, that tranquil state of a soul assured of its salvation through Christ, and so fearing nothing from God and being content with its earthly lot of whatever sort that is, that peace] which transcends all understanding shall garrison {and} mount guard over your hearts and minds in Christ Jesus."*

Once I had made the decision to pursue this tranquil state, the wide spaces of Christ's peace began to open up. I found it to be a remarkably unhurried place. It was a way I had never traveled before. There are no distractions, only the Presence of God, revealing the Lord Jesus Christ. *"Let him turn away from evil and do good; let him seek peace and pursue it"* (1 Peter 3:11 NKJV). This is the only way. It is time to *"think over these things... (understand them and grasp their application) for the Lord will grant you full insight and understanding in everything"* (2 Timothy 2:7) as we garrison and mount a guard over our hearts and minds for Jesus.

3. Appoint yourself judge at the gate of your mind (vs. 8)

> *"For the rest, brethren, whatever is true, whatever is worthy*

of reverence {and} is honorable {and} seemly, whatever is just, whatever is pure, whatever is lovely {and} lovable, whatever is kind {and} winsome {and} gracious, if there is any virtue {and} excellence, if there is anything worthy of praise, think on {and} weigh {and} take account of these things [fix your minds on them]."

A judge always sat at the Gate of the city of Jerusalem. He had records on his table of every person in the city. It was his job to inspect all who passed through the gate. Every person born-again also has this privilege. Jesus has appointed us to sit at the gate of our mind to *'judge'* our own thoughts. We are to vet every thought that enters. We are to sort, analyze, and compare them with the standards of Jesus speaking the Word of God. This is the practical out-working of the Key of SEPARATION.

When we allow toxic, critical or judgmental thoughts to freely access our mind, we have only ourselves to blame for the stress that ensues.

When Jesus told us not to *"judge and criticize and condemn others,* (even ourselves) *so that you may not be judged and criticized and condemned yourselves" (Matthew 7:1),* he was warning us not to express ourselves in prideful judging of others. It is a low habit. Judging others with negative thoughts will always come back to us—in kind. This is the Law of God, written on the hearts of every believer to guide them into right-way-thinking.

A judgment is the *"forming of an opinion, estimate, notion, or conclusion as from circumstances presented to the mind"* (Webster's Dictionary). We assume we have the right to exercise this ability casually and often, even in a hurtful way. Judging others always seeks to put another down in shame and to lift ourselves in pride. We forget the warning issued by Jesus when he said: *"But I tell you, on the Day of Judgment men will have to give account for every idle (inoperative, nonworking) word they speak"* (Matthew 12:36).

Our Father in heaven was specific when He gave *Jesus "authority and granted Him power to execute (exercise, practice) judgment because He is the Son of man"* (John 5:27).When we pass judgment on others we usurp His role as Judge of the Universe! We cannot ever know how the grace of God is working in another's life. Only God does.

When we give up our role as "judge" of others, we let go of our fleshly pride to accept Christ's role as "The Judge." His peace then invades our soul. We have freed ourselves from a powerful destroying stressor.

If we want to be free, we must then apply the 2nd Key of FORGIVENESS, which will then free us of every negative, and align our thinking to the Word of God.

It is not an easy process. It takes effort and diligence to guard our hearts and minds. This is part of the price we pay for being changed into the image of Christ. *"Blessed (happy, fortunate, to be envied) is the man who listens to me, watching daily at my gates, waiting at the posts of my doors"* (Proverbs 8:34). This is the way into Christ's tranquility and long life (Proverbs 3:2).

ACTION PLAN FOR RECOVERY

I Principles

1. God designed us as "receiver" stations for His Word. We were meant to reason with His thoughts, to speak them out, and to act upon them, and to bring them into reality.

2. God's redemptive plan for our fallen minds is *renewal!* Every toxic and negative thought must be recognized, trapped, SEPARATED out and dealt with at the Cross in FORGIVENESS. Negative words break the laws our Lord Jesus has given us to keep our minds at peace.

II Questions

1. *"Satan, as the "father" of lies (John 8:44), has only one weapon—deception! He weaves his lies and half-truths into accusations and hurls them as fiery darts into our minds. He knows our weaknesses and plays into them. Our tendency is then to agree with these suggestions."*

   Can you think of a time when a crisis made you believe the devil's lies? Did you recognize the devastation that came upon you, when you allowed him freedom to speak into your mind? Did the stress affect you physically, emotionally, mentally? How did it affect your relationships? Write it out, so that you *see* what Satan has been trying to do to you.

2. *"These pesky animals (foxes) dart across the front of your mind, chasing each other's tails. They move in packs, hiding along the way, making it hard for you to see them. But once you recognize them, just reach up, snatch them from your mind and break their backs! By asking the Holy Spirit to shine His light upon them, you will see them."*

   Is this a description of your mind when it is stressed out and racing? Are you now ready to hunt these foxes down, to SEPA-RATE them out, and to break their backs? List your thoughts and bring them before God. Ask Him to FORGIVE you for holding them and allowing them free play in your mind.

III Prayer

Father, I never realized how carelessly I have handled my mind. I allowed negative thoughts to pass through the gate of my mind, without seeing their harmful works. I have freely judged and criticized others and myself. Please FORGIVE me. I now see how this practice built stress in me. I also have had ungodly thoughts towards_____ (be specific). I choose to forgive them and release them to You.

Holy Spirit, I give you control of my mind. Help me to keep a guard over my mind and to compare my every thought with the Word of God. More than anything, I desire a clean, peaceful mind to bless others, and to reveal Your Grace and Love to all around me. Thank You, Lord Jesus, Amen.

CHAPTER EIGHT

Smashing your self-images!

*"...and we were in our own sight as grasshoppers,
and so we were in their sight."*
(Numbers 13:33)

*"What is your servant that you should notice
a dead dog as 1 am?"*
(2 Samuel 9:8, NIV)

Of all the stressors I unearthed in my search for peace, self-images revealed themselves to be the most virulent and the most dangerous.

We live in total ignorance of their controlling, mean, obsessive desire to rule. They are the potentates of the soul, making us live according to flickering illusions inspired by Satan. They are the source of incredible stress.

Webster's Dictionary defines *self-image* as *a mental image one has of oneself.* Perfect! It means we conjure pictures about ourselves in our mind. They let us see in graphic form how we view ourselves and how we want others to see us. We are told to develop *"a good self-image,"* but the truth is that all *self-images,* whether good or bad, are irrational expressions of our fallenness! They are all products of *self.*

Making a study of *self-images* led us to help scores of others who came stressed out because they had no idea who they were. Their identity had been entombed in negative *self-images*. Negative images bind toxic emotions, lies, vows, and expectations together, to form these ruffians in the soul.

This is why *self-images* must be understood and destroyed. We pray that reading this chapter will bring a fresh understanding to you of *self-images* and an urgent desire to see them smashed.

DID ADAM HAVE A SELF-IMAGE?

When God convened a meeting in Heaven, He concluded with this statement: *"Let Us make mankind in Our image... So God created man in His own image, in the image and likeness of God He created him"* (Genesis 1:26-27). Did Adam before the Fall possess a *self-image*? The answer is no! Adam was created to reflect the image of God. He was a chosen vessel designed to convey God's love, joy, peace, and humility on earth. His heart and mind were wholly focused on his Creator and friend. This is why he could say: *"It's all about You, Lord."* He was one with God.

But the Fall changed everything. Instead of being one with Christ in divine fellowship, Adam found he could only commune with himself! He felt cut off. Adam had acquired a fallen, human nature that was in every way opposed to God. He had birthed a new image—a destructive image of himself, which reflected his broken relationship with God. Adam had a new refrain: *"It's all about* me, *Lord."*

Did Adam before the Fall possess a self-image? The answer is no! Adam was created to reflect the image God. He was a chosen vessel designed to convey God's love, joy, peace, and humility on earth.

Notice what happened to Adam and Eve in their descent from grace. It all began when they disobeyed God. They ate of the forbidden fruit, and then ran from the Presence of God in FEAR. *"I was afraid,"* Adam said, voicing a negative emotion of Satan, for the first time. With nowhere to go, Adam and Eve hid in the shadows of the tree.

God approached and asked them, *"Where are you?"* Adam confessed, *"I was naked; and I hid myself"* (Genesis 3: 9-10). His heart and mind had developed a *fallen image* out of himself—a **Shame image**, clothed in fear, rejection, and guilt. Neither Adam nor Eve asked for FORGIVENESS, so their descent continued.

God then questioned Adam about his disobedience. Suddenly, pride rose up in Adam and he leapt from the shadows of the tree, swinging at God! *"The woman whom You gave to be with me—she gave me (fruit) from the tree and I ate."* (vs. 12). Blame and aggressiveness overtook him. Self had carved another image in Adam's soul—a **Pride image.**

Adam and Eve left the Garden, each with two images etched in their soul—Shame and Pride. In their fallen world, these two emotions would control whatever they did. If things went wrong, *Shame* would cause them to hide! If they wanted to be seen, *Pride* would elevate their souls, giving them power to be and to do. These two emotions forever shaped their destiny witnessing more to the character of Satan, than God. Adam was in rebellion; he had carved not one but two graven images in his soul, both of which God abhorred:

> *"You shall not make yourself any graven image (to worship it) or any likeness of anything that is in the heavens above, or that is in the earth beneath, or that is in the water under the earth; you shall not bow down yourself to them or serve them."* (Exodus 20:4-5)

WE ALL HAVE TWO SELF-IMAGES!

Mankind emerged from the wonders of Eden, packing a sterile mix of raw negative emotions, *shame* and *pride*, boiling in a sea of fear. In this soulishness, every man, woman and child struggles to compensate for their loss by creating new images in their souls.

This is the root of all stress. We were all born dysfunctional in confusion and iniquity, unable to find answers to the questions: *Who am I and why was I born?* Every person born on planet earth was dropped into this ocean of fear and must struggle for identification. We are no longer God-conscious, but self-conscious. We identify fully with the emotions and thinking of our ancestor—fallen Adam!

Until I saw my own true fallen nature, I was unable to fathom the depth of Christ's love, which took Him to the Cross for me. I first had to see this teeter-totter swing of shame and pride.

Shame would always swing me down into the safety of the tree shadows, to hide when things went wrong. Pride would swing me up, helping me to be seen, to fight for my right to exist. This movement goes on from birth to death, non-stop. There is no escape from this teeter-totter motion, except at the redeeming Cross of Calvary.

God sees these self-images as idols of our *"self-will and unsubmissiveness"* (Ezekiel 14:4). *"For My people have committed two evils: they have forsaken Me, the Fountain of living waters, and they have hewn for themselves cisterns, broken cisterns which cannot hold water" (Jeremiah 2:13).* Self-images live by their own rules, never by the Word of God!

How self-images operate in us

It's like this: When someone hurts us, our *Shame Image* drags us into the dark recesses of life. We wallow there awhile letting our *Shame* beat on us. But we are unable to fathom the source of its power pack of lies: in our *shame*, we feel unclean; we don't like ourselves; what we see and feel is uncomfortable to our senses. So we run to our mental hide-a-way in self-pity.

It is a steep descent, into an uncircumcised, netherworld bearing our *"shame with those who go down into the pit"* (Ezekiel 32:30).

Like Mephibosheth, who descended from the peace of Jerusalem to end up in the waste lands of Lo-Debar, our shame image reminds us constantly of who we think we are: less than human, empty, a "dead dog" (2 Samuel 4:4; and 2 Samuel 9:1-13). Self is our worst enemy!

Then without notice, *Pride* says: *"That's enough! I want out."* We begin the climb from our pit; we need an identity and are willing to strive and fight to get one. This *Pride image* makes us feel we are doing something that's right. We feel positive and suddenly important, believing that self-effort is the way to fulfill our destiny. No wonder we are loathe to give up our *Pride-images*! But take note: The root of all Pride is buried shame, insecurity and guilt, enveloped in fear.

Self-images are primed to rise and fall in seconds, keeping us in a state of anxiety and confusion. Satan often instigates these movements up and down, even prompting one image to fight against the other for supremacy.

When *Shame* rises, our *Pride image* rests: when pride rises, our *Shame image* hides. This constant motion absorbs enormous energy and is highly stressful. This jostling keeps us divided in our minds; we don't know who we are. We feel lost, without purpose, living in a wasteland.

Every emotional and mental ill derives from these vagrant images floating in a sea of fear. Whether, insecurity, depression, despair, guilt, hatred, bitterness, envy or jealousy they all tap into the roots of either our shame or pride images. Every argument and hurt finds its roots in these two images. Self rules willfully from the throne of our hearts, controlling our tendencies to feel either one of these emotions.

If we are to know the peace of God, these images must be deactivated by the power of the Holy Spirit, SEPARATED and brought to the Cross in FORGIVENESS.

How "Self" caused the Prodigal to fall

Jesus illustrated this dysfunctional, swinging feature of man's self nature in the story of the Prodigal Son (Luke 15:11). The Prodigal's *Pride image* whispered that he was missing out on life.

His father's ranch was too small—like a prison; he didn't belong there. There was more to life than this; he would never find fulfillment at home and he wanted out! These dark rumblings were his secret. He would submit to his father's rule only for as long as it suited him.

We are all like the Prodigal! We battle every day with the two fallen images of our self-nature.

The day he confronted his father, all pretense fell away. His *pride*-filled nature rose up before him: *"Father, give me what's mine,"* he said, in a fighting mood. He wanted his inheritance now! He wanted to do his own thing. Prideful attitudes lured him away into the world. He wanted to make a name for himself, to live in comfort, to be someone. But it was all an illusion washed in pride.

Later, far from his father's ranch, instead of fame and fortune he found himself in deep poverty, groveling in a pigpen. His *Shame image* now reared up: he was alone; his money had all gone; his friends had left him and so had his dreams—he felt rejected. All hope had gone. Humiliated and hungry, he ate pig's food. Self-pity overwhelmed him. Suddenly, he longed for the peace of his father's home.

He had allowed *self* to take over and to control his destiny. When he saw the destructive power of his self-images, he realized the emotional pain in him was all **self-inflicted stress**! He looked toward God and confessed: *"I have sinned against heaven and in Your sight."* It was at this point that the wayward son repented and applied the Key of FORGIVENESS, and returned home to the love and peace he remembered in his Father's home.

We are all like the Prodigal! We battle every day with the two fallen *self-images of our self-nature,* just like he did. No one is exempt. Whether in *Shame* or *Pride,* we need to recognize that these images oppose God. They are idols set before Him.

1. SHAME IMAGES ARE STRESSORS

Shame images carry the potential of being powerful stress agents. Their inspired goal is to disrupt our lives—to make us feel we don't belong. It doesn't take much to trigger a *Shame image* to rise in our mind, cutting us with a thousand ragged swords.

I left Grammar school at sixteen, with an ugly *Shame*-filled image of *a failure.* Without knowing it, *Shame* had carved a king-size "inferiority complex" in my soul, which made me hug the shadows of life. Even the most trivial incident caused this image to pop, stirring the same old shame-filled emotions and thoughts. Its lies would pound in my head: *"You can't cope. You're stupid!"* And passively I agreed!

I carried this *failure image* all through my school years. I entered the work force lugging this hardened image on my back, feeling unloved and not knowing who I was. I was a victim, held behind prison bars of *self.*

1. Shame images like to be named

In counseling others we collected names that individuals had attached to their shame images. Each perfectly described how they felt and thought. Every named image carried a powerful message of a dominant pain in their lives.

All through her life, Dana thought of herself as a *"little manikin..."* This image was reinforced by the constant reference of her parents to her—as a *"cute, curly-haired doll."* She felt different from other children. At four, she accepted this image of herself: *"I'm for show, I'm not real. I have to be quiet and stay in the background. It doesn't matter that I don't say anything, as long as others see me as cute."*

She believed she was a doll, who had no purpose other than to be "looked at." By the time she reached her teen years, she had turned away from life, and had filled her heart with anger and resentment. Only after recognizing her image and hanging it on the Cross in FORGIVENESS was she set free.

Here is a list of some named withdrawal *Shame images* we collected. If there is one that fits you, why not circle it?

SHAME IMAGES

Image	Thought triggers
Rag doll	*"I'm a worthless rag doll; no one wants me"*
Pawn	*"I always get pushed around"*
Punching bag	*"Everyone beats on me"*
Wimp	*"I don't fight; I want peace"*
Trash	*"I'm a piece of garbage to throw away"*
Stone	*"I'm a worthless rock, to be sat on, or kicked"*
Block-head	*"Everyone sees me as a stupid empty-head"*
Invisible	*"I don't count; no one sees me anyway"*
Failure	*"I can't do anything right; everything goes wrong"*
A Big Zero	*"I am nothing, a big nobody"*
Dunce	*"I was born stupid –at the bottom of the heap"*

Figure 5. Common Shame images we carry

Notice that each image is constructed out of lies. Lies attach themselves to the image, one by one, over the years with each successive hurt or trauma. Gradually, the image increases its power as sin adds to sin. These attached lies are like whips that lash our senses, especially in crises. Lies cannot be cut and destroyed by natural means—they can be only be axed by the Spirit of God.

Growing up, I felt like a caricature drawn in the ink of shame: *"A punching bag; stupid; a failure!"* These images aptly described the convoluted mix of my emotions and thoughts. Sometimes others would confirm these titles! Their lies screamed all day in my mind, reminding me *I was a nobody!* This self introspection posted huge road blocks along my life-path.

Even after becoming a Christian, these *Shame images*, although weakened by prayer and the Word, held on to their power. They could still launch painful assaults without warning, and hurl me back into the shadows. Their lies could bind me in chains for days. I reasoned that, for as long as these loathsome creatures remained active, *self* would still rule in me. Not until I understood the strategies of the enemy, did I take these *Shame images* to the Cross.

We don't carry just one *shame*-based caricature of ourselves. Images like company! We add new figures to our imaginary family as the pain deepens in us. But multiplying our images also multiplies our fears. This is how multiple personality disorders develop.

2. *Shame images assault us—verbally*

Verbal put-downs are a common failing of personalities weakened by the power of negative images. It is a noxious habit of the fallen soul.

Put-downs are darts hurled out of our subconscious from our *Shame images* into our minds. When things go wrong, we feel we must punish ourselves to atone for our guilt. We fire curses at ourselves, which we have secretly tucked away to punish ourselves for such occasions. Shouting, *"You blockhead!"* to yourself may give you some release from pent-up frustration, but this kind of caustic self-abuse is firmly rooted in a *Shame image*, which lives in perpetual fear of being rejected in the midst of failure or embarrassment. Put-downs are the devil's suggestions and should be recognized for what they are—sin. They are extremely toxic to the mind and shred the immune system.

If our desire is for a healthy mind, we must cultivate more balanced, positive ways to speak to ourselves, particularly in crises. Try statements like these: *"This is really bad, but God is in control. I trust Him to see me through. I cast all my cares upon Him. I am going to have a good day."* Instead of being angry at yourself, or another, speak out positive statements towards those who have hurt you: *"He is having a hard day! I trust God will work things out between us. I believe everything is going to be all right."* Blessing yourself and the one who hurt you will lift off your own pain. It will break this mischievous habit and open heaven's door for you.

Angie came from a well-known family in Trinidad. But her parents were extremely abusive toward her. Her mom ribbed her constantly about her teeth—they showed too much. *"I saw myself every day as deformed."* (She wasn't! This was entirely her perception). *"My mom would scream at me to close my mouth. She was ashamed of the way I looked and made me feel ugly."* Her coping mechanism was to develop well-honed put-downs—curses, which she threw at herself every day: *"I'm an ugly brat. I'm a stupid reject."* Trying to close her mouth became an obsession, fingering her lips to stretch them over her teeth. All the while, she cursed the day she was born. Angie poured out angry judgments towards her mom: *"I hated her so much, I wanted her dead!"*

Chastizing herself eventually drove her into depression and attempted suicide. When Angie became aware of the reason for her self-scolding, her life began to change. She saw her angry judgments toward her mom and herself. Recognition is often a slow-dawning process, but it is the first step in healing.

Eventually, she asked God to FORGIVE her for the shame she had put on herself, so needlessly. She FORGAVE her mom and, for the first time, was able to cultivate a close relationship with her. A year later, we heard she had become involved in her church and was experiencing real joy in Christ for the first time. This is the power behind FORGIVENESS!

2. PRIDE IMAGES ARE STRESSORS

Every person needs to feel significant—to have a purpose in life. We all have this built-in need: we long for others to see and admire us.

Art Matthias points out in his book *Biblical Foundations of Freedom* (Thomaston, Georgia: Pleasant Valley Publications, 2000, page 142), that the latent fear of being shamed and rejected creates an enormous urge to fabricate a new identity for ourselves. We construct aggressive *Pride images* of ourselves in order to fight for our right to be in the world—just as Adam did.

Pride images cause us to strive for love, acceptance, and respect, and we work hard to get it. Workaholics, take note! You may be burning out for the wrong reasons. *Pride images* are similar to *Shame-based images*, in that they are bathed in fear. *Pride images* are hard to detect and even harder to give-up. Why? Because we like them! They make us feel good, important and in control.

I had always sought loner occupations, with minimal contact with a boss! I wanted to work on my own. My first job was in the jungles of Borneo—far from peering eyes! This was later followed by a 20-year foray in the ivory-tower equity research establishments in Montreal and Toronto, walking its hallowed halls virtually alone, complete with my own office, car, and itinerary! Without realizing it, I had landed in a hot-bed environment of Type A's. Driven to succeed, along with my peers, I entered into several work disciplines, and carved a pathway to satisfy a deep *Self* need to be recognized and loved. I had no idea I was cultivating an image that God abhorred.

In my *Pride*, I sought to please others and be perfect. Inherently, this combination makes for a brittle character and unstable relationships. The undercarriage of my newfound personality proved rickety. Always lurking in the shadows of my mind, ready to pounce was a writhing, hoary *Shame image*. Inner expectations tugged constantly in self condemnation: *"One day, they will find you out!"* Subtle temptations would fly around my mind: *"Reject them before they reject you! Don't get hurt again."*

1. Pride images like to be named

Just as it was a revelation to find *Shame images* had names, I was even more amazed to find that *Pride images* also carried descriptive monikers. Below are some we collected from our counseling. In each case, the counselee expressed surprise and sadness at the size of the dead weights they had carried around with them for no purpose at all! They had named their images without even knowing it!

PRIDE IMAGES

Images	Thought triggers
Controller	*"I must be in control; the boss"*
Corrector	*"I must correct everyone's faults"*
Poor Nun	*"I must be poor to show I'm spiritual"*
Mr. Fix-it	*"I'm the only one who can fix-it"*
Macho	*"I'm one tough dude"*
Nice Guy	*"I want everyone to like me"*
Know it all	*"I know; you don't"*
Sick man	*"I must be sick to get attention"*
Forecaster	*"I know what's to come"*
Pundit	*"I must be first with the news"*

Figure 6. Common Pride images we carry

2. Pride images turn us into 'performers and perfectionists'

Pride will try to cover a deep sense of shame and unworthiness within by prompting us to excel in life, often in extraordinary ways. In an attempt to rescue a low self-worth, pride demands we please others and be perfect to gain their love and acceptance. Such people are forced into acting their parts: *"If I do this perfectly, they will love me."* Their lives are dictated by inner lies; obvious words punctuate their vocabulary:

*"I **should** have done better!"*
*"I **must** get this done!"*
*"I **have** to do it now!"*
*"If it is going to be done right, I **ought** to do it!"*

Dana also had a *Pride* side to her doll image.

"I saw myself as a doll: perfect and absolutely flawless! I acted out the part to the letter. My clothes had to be the best, and every wrinkle was a nightmare! A stain would send me into a fit! Every hair had to be in place, even on windy days. I thought everyone expected me to be perfect. When others corrected me, I became rigid and resentful; they no longer saw me as perfect! I had to be perfect, and any doubt would send me back into shame, wanting to do nothing in my hiding place. The stress of living up to these high -expectations eventually took its toll. I worried and became anxious about pleasing others and appearing perfect. Eventually, I had to take anti-depressants to curb my mood swings." As Dana SEPARATED out her two images and applied the Key of FORGIVENESS, peace came into her life.

People like Dana strive for love. Finding an identity in a loveless home is immensely stressful. For her, seeds of bitter roots developed prideful coping mechanisms, which led her to perform for others as *"perfect."* Later in life, her body reacted in stress, depression, and sickness. Both images operated out of her subconscious mind. As she applied the Key of Forgiveness to these controlling powers, both were placed on the Cross. Whenever she had problems with them, she knew exactly what to do.

Perfectionists impose tremendous burdens upon themselves and others. They often find it hard to get close to others. Some find it very difficult to delegate even minor tasks, and may become angry when it's not done *"just right."* Frustration levels are always high since few people can meet their standards. They are unable to see the difference between *"good enough"* and *"perfect."* Dr. Eliot points out in his book that the difference between the two *"is a logarithmic increase in effort"* (ibid, page 138).

Christian leaders, especially of Type A, are prone to perfectionist attitudes. Some are *driven* in their need to appear successful. To bolster their image of success, their church projects must be bigger and more exciting than the last. An inner cry from childhood continually whispers in their souls: *"If I do this well, they will love me."*

Inevitably, disappointments, offences, and frustrations mount. Their emotional teeter-totter then swings downwards from *Pride* to *Shame*. They crash, often hard, into rejection and guilt. If perfectionist attitudes are not dealt with, such people become candidates for burn out, panic attacks, and the hospital.

Self is the master designer of our images. It knows how to render a personality weak and brittle. But it is all self-inflicted stress.

The Apostle Peter experienced these rapid up and down emotional swings. His *Pride image* slipped suddenly into his *Shame image* many times in his life, before his life-changing experience at Pentecost.

This volatility is best seen when Jesus told the disciples they would all be offended and fall away (Matthew 26:33-34). Peter's *Pride image* rose aggressively with an opinion: *"I will never do so"* he said, blurting it out. Jesus replied by saying that he would deny Him three times. It happened. After Peter had uttered his three self-condemning denials in the court of Caiaphas, he recalled Jesus' prophetic words. Suddenly, his *Pride image* plunged and his *Shame image* rose to take over, overwhelming him with self-pity and depression. He wept bitterly as he left the courtyard. The change in his image from up to down had taken place without warning, in an instant.

Gord flipped back and forth in his life, from *a nobody,* in frustration and despair, to a *sophisticated urbanite* in a matter of days. These emotional swings began as a child in his desperate attempt *to be someone* in the family.

To find an identity, he imagined himself in various career roles, each carrying an image of one who had expertise and strong opinions in particular disciplines. One time he saw himself as a budding politician, at another a computer geek, then a literary critic, a learned philosopher, and a professor of religion. He really didn't know who he was. For a period, these named images would help lift his spirits, to cover earlier childhood wounding. But a single put-down from his boss, dad or wife, would be all it would take for his *Pride image* to crumble and for his *Shame image* to raise. Once again he would withdraw, feeling hurt, and a *nobody*.

His downers loaded him with acute loneliness and self-condemnation. These swings, eventually, weakened his immune system. Late in life, he become a Christian and submitted to counseling. The swings stopped and his stressor images lost their power to inflict pain. His new image in Christ began to stabilize his personality, and the swinging stopped. At last, he was seeing who he really was, a child of the living God.

Most of us loathe giving up our *Pride images.* They are our identity; self has made them. We set them on high groves in our minds—as **idols** (2 Kings 17:12 KJV) giving them all our attention.

When we realize how we have spent all our lives carefully cultivating our Pride images, only to find they are worthless in God's sight, air starts to come out of our balloon!

> **When we realize how we have spent all our lives carefully cultivating our Pride images, only to find they are worthless in God's sight, air starts to come out of our balloon!**

Prideful people must lead in conversations to declare their identity. They must feel like they are making a contribution and so ready their opinions for every opportunity. Opinions are the air that fills the *Pride image* balloon. But so easily and quickly the balloon is punctured like Gord's. *"By pride and insolence comes only contention, but with the well- advised is skillful and godly wisdom"* (Proverbs 13:10). *"Pride goes before destruction and a haughty spirit before a fall"* (Proverbs 16:18). Where there is pride, shame is guaranteed to follow: *"When swelling and pride come, then emptiness and shame come also"* (Proverbs 11:2).

When pride works secretly in an individual providing a *religious* cover to early childhood rejection the manifestations can be bizarre, but extremely difficult for the victim to recognize. Practicing *religion* rather than faith is a way self expresses the pride-filled aggression of Adam's fallen nature. Religion fosters blaming, criticism, judgmen-talism and legalitistic thinking. Only in deep humility before the Lord is this work of the flesh broken at the Cross. Pride always sows its own seeds of shame: *"In the fool's own mouth is a rod (to shame) his pride"* (Proverbs 14:3).

Pride makes a cruel master of its images.

DE-FANG YOUR SELF-IMAGES

The gateway to a stress-free life in Christ is by way of an intense hunger for righteousness, and an all-consuming desire to change into the image of Jesus Christ.

Christians everywhere are emerging from the shadows of rejec-tion and fear of failure having de-fanged their self-images, nailing them on the Cross. They are taking their rightful place as champi-ons for Christ as leaders in every field, doing exploits for Jesus until He comes. Their fallen self-images are being destroyed on the Cross. They are learning to live in the resurrection power of Jesus Christ, displaying His Life and character to the world around them (John 1:12).

De-fanging our images does not have to take long, but it does take courage and prayer. The most important part of the exercise is to bring our images into Christ's Light.

They must be SEPARATED from the darkness, plucked up, rooted out and destroyed as 'other gods' (Micah 5:14). We must take responsibility for them and reckon them dead. For too long they have fogged our thinking, discernment, and sound judgment. Our self-images have influenced, and even controlled our behavior, causing us to heed their raucous demands, rendering us passive to the still small voice of God within.

Then we de-fang our images through confession, FORGIVE-NESS and repentance before God.

We must always be on our guard to check these rising stars of self at the gate of our mind. Remember, *"Greater is He that is in you than he that is in the world"* (1 John 4:4, KJV). By faith we can cause them to submit to the new management of the Holy Spirit dwelling in us.

Affirm yourself in Christ

Our heavenly Father has already laid out for us in Scripture how to do it. *"Clothe yourselves therefore, as God's own chosen ones...[put on] love {and} enfold yourselves with the bond of perfectness...and let the peace (soul harmony which comes) from Christ rule (act as umpire continually) in your hearts"* (from Colossians 3:12-15).

Self seeks to dominate at the smallest pretext. Memorizing positive affirmations about ourselves and by speaking them hundreds of times a day if necessary, will gradually banish them, allowing the Holy Spirit to assume control. Here are some affirmations you should carry with you on cue cards. Gradually they will build your new identity in Christ.

MY IDENTITY IN CHRIST

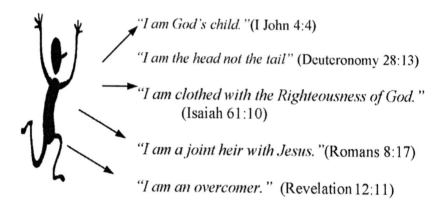

"I am God's child." (I John 4:4)

"I am the head not the tail" (Deuteronomy 28:13)

"I am clothed with the Righteousness of God." (Isaiah 61:10)

"I am a joint heir with Jesus." (Romans 8:17)

"I am an overcomer." (Revelation 12:11)

Figure 7. Developing your identity in Christ

This is how we renew our minds and hearts. His Word becomes a powerful defensive shield. *"We all, with unveiled face, beholding as in a mirror the glory of the Lord, are being transformed into the same image from glory to glory, just as by the Spirit of the Lord"* (2 Corinthians 3:18, NKJV).

As we change, we are infused with a new sense of belonging and joy. We feel more balanced, with Jesus at the center of our lives. All worry and anxiety drain from us as we become more settled and rooted in Christ's life. The Lord is calling every saint to this Way of Life. *"Be well balanced (temperate, sober of mind}, be vigilant and cautious at all times; for the enemy of yours, the devil, roams around like a lion roaring (in fierce hunger) seeking someone to seize upon and devour"* (1 Peter 5:8).

This sense of being *balanced* enables us to feel the same today, as yesterday and tomorrow. There is a constancy that flows from Christ through us, that isn't dependent upon the weather, money in the bank, or a promotion. As we renew our minds, our spiritual keel steadies in rough waters, and our sails open. Instead of listening to our circumstances for guidance, we become listeners for the voice of the Holy Spirit. Our new sense of balance is entirely based upon a person—our Lord and Savior, Jesus Christ.

Paul exhorts us to set our minds on things above (Colossians 3:2). We are to fix our gaze upon Jesus (Hebrews 12:2) in order to perfect our faith. When we revert to being self-absorbed, we sink into double-mindedness and stress. Our inner life with its renewed mind always reflects in our outer life (Proverbs 23:7).

The more we deal with these inner monsters through FORGIVE-NESS, the more Christ's peace will flow in us and out to others. We are then able to fully align ourselves to God and enter into His rest. All striving is gone. We no longer are tempted to worry and be anxious for tomorrow. We keep our dial tuned to the highly positive side of Jesus *"Your people will offer themselves willingly in the day of Your power"* (Psalms 110:3). This is why James urges us to *"Draw near to God and He will draw near to you. Cleanse your hands, you sinners and purify your hearts"* (James 4:8, NKJV).

When we reckon our self-images dead, we have fully aligned ourselves to God and His Word.

When we reckon our self-images dead, we have fully aligned ourselves to God and His Word.

As you begin to destroy your self-images, you will notice subtle changes take place in you—silently but effectively. Your outlook on life will steadily improve; you will enjoy greater calmness in difficult situations and a richer sense of fellowship with Jesus. This is God's way to renew your mind and spirit (Psalms 51:10) *"until Christ is completely and permanently formed (molded) within you"* (Galatians 4: 19).

ACTION PLAN FOR RECOVERY

I Principles

1. The Fall split man's personality—we now have two images: a *Shame image* and a *Pride image.* Both compete with one another in fear. Control and elimination of these images can only be accomplished through the process of SEPARATION and FORGIVENESS.

2. Images are a product of *self.* God sees them as idols, occupying high places in our minds. They are stress makers and potentially damaging to our health.

II Question

Are you now ready to plot your images? If your answer is yes then sit before the Lord and ask Him to help you draw your own self-images. You will find the two at first hopelessly jumbled together, creating a lot of confusion. But once you begin the process of SEPARATING first your emotions and then your thoughts your images will emerge before you!

Track down the thoughts that are attached to your *Shame image* and write them in on the figure below. Do the same with your *Pride image.* Try to name your images.

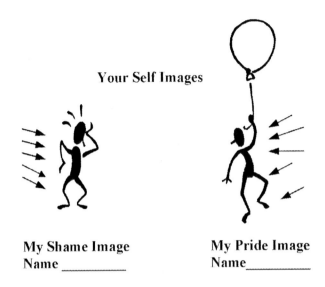

Your Self Images

My Shame Image   My Pride Image
Name _____   Name_____

Figure 8. Plotting your Shame and Pride images

As you SEPARATE out your two images, step back to look objectively at them. You will no doubt be aghast at the monsters you have been lugging around in your mind—for no purpose!

III Prayer

Father, I thank You for allowing me to see and SEPARATE out my Shame and Pride images. I want them destroyed on the Cross. I now bring them before You in confession. I developed a Shame image called_____ and a Pride image called_____. Unknown to me they became idols within me. Please FORGIVE me. They separated me from You and from those I love. No longer will I carry them in me and nurture them. By faith I reckon them dead. They will no longer direct what I feel and what I am to think. I choose You Jesus to be my Lord (Galatians 2:20) and I will affirm myself daily using Your Word, even carrying them around with me. Holy Spirit, begin creating in me the image of Jesus Christ, starting today. Amen.

CHAPTER NINE

Eliminating Your Dangerous Imaginations

*"Because when they knew {and} recognized Him as God,
they did not honor {and} glorify Him as God or give Him
thanks. But instead they became futile {and} godless in
their thinking [with vain imaginings, foolish reasoning,
and stupid speculations] and their senseless
minds were darkened."*
(Romans 1: 21)

There exists a large body of people in the Church of Jesus Christ who see no need to change the way they feel, think, or how they use their imagination. *"There is nothing more I can do. I am free, already changed into His image. The Cross did it all for* me."

I owned this party-line for years, until it emerged as a monstrous lie. I had carried my stressed-out mind across the divide from darkness into Christ's glorious light, without ever once believing that the Holy Spirit could play a role in the government of my emotions, thoughts, and imagination.

God gave us an *imagination* to create reality. Imaging is the act of forming mental pictures in the mind. If you desire a rock garden beneath your front window, you first *see* it! You plan with your imagination how you will do it. You bring it into reality as you speak it out. This is God's way.

If you are a worrier, you are using your imagination in a wrong way. Energy is being drawn from you unnecessarily. You have allowed your mind to picture what might happen tomorrow, next week or three years away. You are detailing the future negatively through the expectations of your imagination. This is not the way God intended for us to use this precious gift.

All children like to entertain goblins, fairies, and saber-toothed tigers in their fantasy world, but they grow out of the practice by the time they enter public school. A child's imagination is used to create live theatre performances in the mind. He is usually the principle actor. Use of this capacity to imagine is needed for development in early childhood. But when the practice carries into later years as fantasy, it may indicate unresolved traumas and deep issues in the soul.

Imagination without restraint leads into fantasy. Fantasies are a form of mind pleasure, in which time is suspended for the purpose of self-gratification.

WHY WE CULTIVATE EVIL IMAGINATIONS

Our imagination is a gift of God, but if it remains unredeemed *self* continues to direct. *Self* causes our imagination to drift aimlessly, often into fear, and we have no idea why. Most of our negative picture making in our minds derives from a low estimation we have of ourselves. What we feel and think about ourselves is transformed into colorful graphics, which hide in our subconscious. They rise up in our minds without our permission; but when we look at our filming objectively, we see them as empty and vain. We've never been taught that this practice is sin, nor how we are to use our imaginations correctly—for the Lord Jesus Christ.

Did you know it takes just as much energy to see good things as it does the bad? Few ever learn that secret. In our fear-filled, negative world, our imaginations are too preoccupied with worry. Instead of being a blessing, this gift of God becomes a high voltage stressor.

We view life through our imaginations. We picture its every step. Most people, however, see only negative situations through their imaginations.

Our body responds automatically to what we feel and think. It is unable to distinguish between what is real and what is unreal, or between truth and a lie. This is why it is important to SEPARATE out every negative emotion and thought, and to compare them with the standards set for us by Jesus Christ. A broken rear axle or zero bank account plays on the mind with pictures of failure and poverty. Our imagination soars into unreality and the body is affected. But God warns us not to walk according to the imaginations emanating from our evil hearts (Jeremiah 18:11-12). Worries, anxiety, and fretting are all components of a negatively inspired mind and heart. As born-again believers, we now have the opportunity to redeem our imagination for Jesus and to bring this volatile element of the mind into peace.

FANTASIZING IS DANGEROUS!

Imagination without restraint leads into fantasy. Fantasies are a form of mind pleasure, in which time is suspended for the purpose of self-gratification. They are intensely personal, secretly embraced, and extremely stressful to the brain and body. Unredeemed imaginations of this kind are fertile soil for the work of demons. All are abominations before God.

We have seen many individuals caught in these ungodly webs. In each case, they were unaware of the powers of the strongholds to inflict serious stressful pain. When the fantasies were brought into the Light, the individuals were horrified at the ugliness they had nurtured in their minds for years.

Fantasizing is different from an image. Images, which we talked about in Chapter eight, tend to be pictures we hang before our minds about ourselves. Fantasies, on the other hand are *movies* developed in the recesses of our minds, in which we are the director, scriptwriter, choreographer, and principal actor. Through them, we portray ourselves and project into the future.

In my early years, fantasizing was my refuge. Creating vivid movies in my mind was my escape to dull the pain of rejection and loneliness. As a schoolboy, day-dreaming got me into a lot of trouble! One teacher told my parents: *"I could throw a paper ball at him and he still wouldn't wake up!"* I could sit for hours on a white rock, in front of our house, oblivious to all around me, passively wiling away the hours locked in my dream world. It was a vibrant, colorful universe of adventure, exploration and escape, all of which I controlled!

It was revelation to find just how harmful this practice can be. Even a one-minute flight into the world of fantasy stresses the soul. This self-immolation not only distorts reality in the mind, but also stunts personal development. If left alone without restraints, fantasizing can become an overbearing taskmaster which seeks to control the body and mind.

We need to see this practice as God does—as sin. Any temptation to daydream should prompt immediate confession and repentance. After a short time of resisting this dangerous practice, daydreaming or fantasizing will never bother you in the same way again. You will have your guard up.

Here are some of the more common fantasy habits we identified in our counseling:

- Hero fantasizing
- Escaping dramas
- Romantic flights into fantasy
- Fear inducing fantasies
- Adventure imaging
- Religious fantasies
- Revenge fantasies

• Sexual fantasies

Fantasies gradually poison the mind in secret, but sooner or later, they will find you out. Below are some we studied in depth:

1. *Fantasizing fearful scenes*

Creating fear-inducing fantasies is a common practice, especially among children. If carried over to adult life, they inflict serious stress.

Susie, age 10, identified with a character in the story she was reading. It filled her with grief and distress. She read of a little girl who couldn't stop running down a steep slope. The dad in the story watched her and yelled: *"Fall down!"* The girl obeyed her dad's call just in time and was saved from going over the cliff edge.

But Susie wove her own sequel to the scene. She saw herself running like the little girl down the hill. Then her imagination took over. When her dad yelled "*fall down*," she saw herself still running toward the cliff edge. She couldn't stop. Full of fear, she saw herself hurtling over the cliff face.

This vivid sequel played upon her through her teen years to adulthood. No matter how hard she tried, this same tormenting scene would often pound her mind. Each time the same question surfaced: "Why *didn't you obey your dad?"* She had become enslaved to this fantasy and to the question. The devil had taken advantage of an open door.

Counseling revealed an inner reluctance to obey her dad. She held bitter resentments against him. She believed he didn't really love her and at times seemed out to hurt and embarrass her. She never felt protected, so felt no obligation to obey him. When Susie SEPARATED out her negative feelings and thoughts and asked FORGIVENESS for not honoring her dad, at last her childhood book was closed.

Peace came when she chose not to be led by her imagination. It was revelation to see how this latent negative power in her mind could introduce so much fear and guilt into her life. As an adult and a Christian, her greatest fear was disobeying God, especially if He asked her to do something difficult. She thought she would disobey Him as she had her dad. When she renounced this practice before God, she found herself moving into a new level of strength and peace in God.

2. Fantasizing romantic, historical figures

Cultivating images of this kind may seem harmless, even noble, but there is always a cost. Imprinting some fascinating figure from the past in your subconscious mind, and seeking to live out the image, will inevitably replicate that life, for good or evil.

Saddam Hussein coupled his destiny to King Nebuchadnezzar, playing the King in his subconscious imagination. What we now know is that even some of the finer details of Nebuchadnezzar's life were duplicated in the life of the Iraqi President.

The golden image of Nebuchadnezzar, erected on the plain of Dura, turned out to be top heavy and fell. Saddam Hussein had his own image erected in the Baghdad town square. That too toppled ignominiously!

The King, doing penance in the Palace grasslands, was found to have grown nails like corkscrews and hair like birds feathers (Daniel 4:33). Saddam Hussein, pulled from a hole in the Babylonian desert, similarly revealed long twisted nails and hair matted like those of a bird!

A well-known Canadian press baron cultivated an image of Napoleon from childhood. He developed mindsets that imitated the "glorious past" in that person, even making decisions for his own business empire like the military commander from a stool once owned by Napoleon. Like Napoleon, at the pinnacle of worldly success and power, he fell. His business empire unraveled as the negative, destructive seeds planted in his imagination from his youth reaped a whirlwind of high stress and devastation in his own ruinous Waterloo!

God tells us from His Word, that use of our imagination for vain purposes is not a part of life, but a withdrawal from it into passivity (Romans 1:21). Empty imaginations conflict with Christ's true nature and purposes. They are sin, and the consequences are always the same—SELF-INFLICTED STRESS.

3. Fantasizing with revenge.

Christians are not exempt from this vain process. The number one enemy in the Church today is giving and taking offences. All grudges are the product of self-inflicted evil imaginings. Zechariah points this out when he said: *"Let none of you devise or imagine or think evil against his brother in your heart"* (Zechariah 7: 10). A judgment, a critical remark, or bitter feelings is processed in toxic imaginations, which whirl across the mind.

Watching a brother being pulled down into destruction in your mind is a sin! *"Do not contrive or dig up, or cultivate evil against your neighbor"* (Proverbs 3:29). Cruel imaginings like these in the secret recesses of the mind are potent seed stressors, which inevitably reap harvests of destruction.

Tommy grew up with a seven-year-old heart locked in a man's body. As a prank, the seven-year-old, jumped onto the bumper of a truck, speeding along a country road. *"The driver spotted me, stopped the vehicle and in a fit screamed at me. He turned me upside down and plunged my head repeatedly into an ice covered pool of water."* The shock scarred the boy for life.

From that time on, all authority figures were suspect. *"I visualized doing the same thing to him—and worse. All I wanted was vengeance. My hate turned me into a loner. At school, I rebelled and failed all grades."*

As a chronic introvert, Tommy grew up barely able to form

words in his mouth. Sexual fantasizing and self-gratification became his only outlet. *"It made me feel important. At least I had control over something!"* Jobs lasted about a year, most ending with angry upsets with the boss. To survive, he cultivated a prideful spirit of independence: *"No one is going to tell me what to do! I am my own boss."*

Memories of the brute treatment never left his subconscious mind. Internalizing his hateful desire for revenge produced stressors that eventually compromised his immune system and ravaged his body. By the time he had reached forty, he manifested debilitating heart, lung, and bowel problems.

Even after Tommy came to Christ, these powerful stressors still held him in bondage. Not until he saw the rage and revenge in his heart, did the bitter chains around his soul loosen. Peace began to flood his soul. Health returned to his body and he was able to find true fulfillment in his local church and hold down a job.

4. Fantasizing sex

Like many addictions, this kind of fantasizing possesses a wake that seems always to lead back to the ship called *shame* that floats without controls on an ocean of fear, guilt and rejection.

Without dealing with the root cause of this problem, sexual fantasizing cannot be healed, only suppressed. This addiction sugarcoats a superficial need for a love substitute. It creates a momentary feeling that *"I am my own boss."* But lurking under the heart is a loaded gun, with a finger ready to shoot its lies: *"No one accepts me and loves me. Without a release I'm worthless."*

Medical science now tells us, that powerful chemicals are released in the brain, when minds fantasize with porn images. They hijack the

brain, just as powerfully as heroin.

Medical science now tells us, that powerful chemicals are released in the brain when minds fantasize with porn images. They hijack the brain, just as powerfully as heroin. The temptation to *"look again"* is all that is needed to trigger their release. But the chemicals don't just go away. They linger for months, even years, creating unwanted flashbacks in the mind.

When our imagination is used for vain, empty purposes like this, great stress is imposed on the mind and body. Porn imaging declares the works of the devil. As a result, God's people perish for lack of this knowledge. Habitual involvement in such sinful mind games invites a spirit of insanity to walk into the heart. Satan has a legal right to destroy the mind and body of the saint. *"For it is a land of images, and they are made mad over idols (objects of terror in which they foolishly trust)"* (Jeremiah 50:38).

The Internet has worsened the problem. In the US, pornography is a massive $12 billion a year industry. Streams of this kind of satanic filth have invaded every aspect of society, including the Church, even infecting Church leadership. Internet access is affordable and anonymous. This situation presents an ideal combination for those drawn into lasciviousness. Porn leaves no tracks, no marks (people think!), and is free! Addicts may spend as much as 40-50 hours per week, surfing through thousands of porn sites on the web. They live secret lives, shackled by their evil imaginings, living in fear of being caught.

Fantasizing is one of the best-kept secrets in the Body of Christ. It is an intensely personal addiction, which for some might appear innocent and enjoyable—it bothers no one. As one man told me: *"Porn is a part of me...it is who I am!"* Altar calls for sexual fantasies are known to have convicted as many as a third of the men in a congregation—all hooked on pornography. Fantasizing possesses addictive powers that demand bigger and bigger doses to maintain a high. The victim is gradually lowered by demons into dangerous, socially deviant patterns.

Only as these imaginations are brought before Christ, can they be seen for what they are—idolatry. Ezekiel the prophet broke through the Temple wall to reveal the unrestrained fantasies of the elders. Ugly frescoes were painted on the inner walls of the *"chambers of* (their) *imageries,"* (Ezekiel 8:12, KJV). These backslidden elders had grossed out their fantasies in paint!

This is the equivalent of painting the walls of our souls with the evil imaginations of our depraved thinking. *"The children of Israel did secretly those things that were not right against the Lord their God and they built (images) high places in all their cities ... And they burnt incense in all the high places (worshipped them),* as *did the heathen."* (2 Kings 17: 9-11, KJV).

Jim's granddad and dad were both violent alcoholics. Their lives were pock- marked with destructive episodes of rage and drinking. Porn magazines were left carelessly around the home, which Jim found and picked up. One night, his dad was caught drunk with a prostitute in a local bar. Jim's world unraveled to the last thread. He grew up loathing the alcohol and pornographic fantasizing, which had destroyed his dad.

"But I grew up doing the very same thing (Romans 2:1). *My imagination was caught in a deadly trap.* After he married, he followed his dad's habits into drinking, and developed an insatiable appetite for porn magazines. *"I got saved and rose in leadership in our church. But the pain of rejection was still there, and so was my lust. I felt too ashamed to seek the pastor's help."* In his deep lows, he would visit the local massage parlor for sex, only to return home with a *"heavy load of shame and guilt that took a week or more to lift."* When his strong hateful judgments against his dad were found, he brought the whole mess to the Cross. The stronghold of fantasies in his mind was pulled down and washed in the blood of the Lamb. He never again visited a massage parlor. His imagination came under new management.

The Psalmist tells us we are *shapen in iniquity* (Psalms 51:5, KJV). It requires a measure of humility to see the unrestrained power of our imaginations.

Fantasies build around hurts in the soul. In our woundedness we gravitate to walking in our own counsels, chained by fear, shame, rejection and guilt. *"But they hearkened not, nor inclined their ear, but walked in the COUNSELS and in the IMAGINATION of their evil heart, and went backward, and not forward"* (Jeremiah 7:24, KJV, Emphasis added). We need to see the nature of our fallen imaginations and prayerfully seek to redeem it from abusive self-inflictions.

One man we counseled said this: *"Dwelling under the cloak of a false imagination pulls enormous amounts of energy from me to the point I feel ill."* We need to discern what is godly imagining and what is false. If we fail to make this SEPARATION, we sow seeds of distress in our immune system.

BUILDING A GODLY IMAGINATION

It is time the Church took back the reins of imagination from the control of the flesh and the devil. In one small church, I preached a message on the right use of "our imagination," submitted to the Holy Spirit. I was surprised by the reaction of a few. One said to me afterwards: *"Imagination* is *nothing more than an undisciplined mind."* Another said: *"Using our imagination borders on the New Age. It is not faith!"*

Our God-given imagination is meant to be used for His glory. Mention of the subject should not bring fear of cultic meditation, visualization, and other metaphysical practices. The devil has stolen this gift of God and placed it in his camp. It is time, as believers, we broke the back of this fear and claimed back this gift for God. If we fail to capture our imaginations for Jesus, it will capture us in passivity, negativity, and numbness.

Renew your imagination

Start with the hope of Jesus in you: *"Now faith is the substance of things hoped for, the evidence of things not seen"* (Hebrews 11:1, KJV). Hope in Christ is the most positive projection there is, which we should freely express through our imaginations. When our imaginings are wrapped in His Word, by faith and in love, we are able to build and create.

We operate the same principle God used in Creation. We simply see in our imagination the results of our request placed before Jesus and by faith it is done!

A distraught Mother sees her unsaved daughter caught up in drugs. Ugly scenes of disaster flash through her mind. How does she stop the descent into panic? She must wash her imagination with the Blood of Jesus and the Water of the Word. As she senses Christ's peace over the situation, in faith she must *imagine* her daughter free from *drugs*, and seeing her hands raised in surrender to God.

Victory comes through the eyes of our faith in the Spirit, when *"we do not look at the things which are seen, but at the things which are not seen"* (2 Corinthians 4:18, NKJV). Success does not occur immediately; it takes time for these new seed-pictures to grow. Here are examples of where we may use our redeemed imaginations for Jesus:

- leading someone to Jesus
- performing an act of kindness
- picturing health coming into your body
- seeing yourself before a crowd leading worship or preaching
- seeing your spouse and children healed and saved, and being blessed by God
- seeing prosperity and abundance coming into your hands for the Lord's work

Our capability to imagine is open-ended. The Church is being challenged to put away the foolish imaginations of a child, and to awaken to our responsible use of this Gift. Jesus said: *"He is able to do only what He sees the Father doing"* (John 5:19). What was He doing? He was employing His Spirit to see in His imagination the works of the Father, which He then brought into reality through His

Word and hands.

Take for example the familiar promise in God's Word: *"And my God will liberally supply (fill to the full) your every need according to His riches in glory in Christ Jesus"* (Philippians 4:19). Meditate upon these words for a few moments. *See* every difficult circumstance from this point on as opportunities for God to solve— not you! By faith believe that God will quicken your imagination to see solutions. Build your life upon His visions and dreams in order to do exploits

Begin to cross over the bridge of the natural realm into the spiritual. *See* with your redeemed imagination, washed in the blood of the Lamb, those needs being met in detail by the hand of our Lord. Be bold and courageous to hold your expectations before God, no matter the stormy winds that may blow filling your mind with doubt. This is how we overcome the world, flesh, and the devil.

Repeat Philippians 4:19 not just once a week, but with determination every few moments, if necessary, until the supply is in your hands. *"Let them say continually, 'Let the Lord be magnified, who has pleasure in the prosperity of His servant'* (Psalm 35:27, NKJV)

It makes a difference where you set the bar of your expectations. If your expectations are mostly negative it is time to raise the bar into high positive territory. God will not do it for you. You must be the one with the determination to do it!

Expectations are always bound up with our imaginations. Godly expectations must always be grounded in the Promises of God and tightly wrapped in the positive images we construct in our mind.

Activate the Promises of God through your expectations and imaginative thinking. By faith believe and see *"your youth, (being) renewed, is like the eagle's (strong, overcoming, soaring)!"* (Psalm 103:5). See yourself by faith with knowledge and wisdom coming to you, sufficient to get the task the Lord has assigned to you completed. Aim for a long life to finish the work God has set for you to do. The more of His Promises you commit to your spirit, the greater will be your expectations that God in His mercy and grace will abundantly supply for you in every area of your life. You cannot overdose on God's medicine. His Promises need to be fed by our faith-filled imagination—daily.

God delights in an active imagination that belongs to Him. We begin to see as He sees! It is wonderfully energizing and freeing!

ACTION PLAN FOR RECOVERY

I Principles

1. God gave us an *imagination* to create reality. *Self* hates reality and Truth, so draws our imaginations into creating dark, unreal fantasies.

2. Great stress is placed on the body and the mind when we use our imaginations to worry. A drifting imagination will quickly move into destructive stressor fantasies.

3. God desires that we harness our imaginations for Him. Under His guidance we will be able to use our gift to benefit others, ourselves, and His Kingdom. Without His vision being imparted to us, we perish.

II Questions

1. *"God gave us an imagination to create reality."*

Do you agree with this statement? Does your imagination work against you, making you anxious and fearful? Try to write down what happens in your imagination when you next experience worry. Does the picture making in your mind run into fantasy? Stand back, look, and see them for what they are—sin. Write out your confession as though you were speaking to God.

2. *"Fantasizing further pulls our minds away from reality. It locks into self. It is a form of mind-pleasure, in which time is suspended for the purpose of self-gratification."*

How do your evil-imaginations separate you from God? Look up the scripture 1 Corinthians 13:11. What is God asking you to do with your childish thinking?

3. *"It is time the Church took back the reins of imagination from the control of the flesh and the devil."*

Have you ever asked the Holy Spirit to take over the reins of your imagination, to use it for His glory? Will you do it now?

III Prayer

Father, I confess to You that I have never considered giving You my imagination. I have always allowed my imagination to drift aimlessly, often into sin. I never realized that it controlled me and is inspired by the devil. Please FORGIVE me for the way I have used my imagination. I see now it has worked havoc in me and has even worked against my relationship with You, my family and others. Cover my imagination, I pray, with Your precious blood, and cleanse it from all unrighteousness (1 John 1:9). Impart to me, I pray, your vision and dreams and help me to use my imagination to bring glory to You and Your work. I pray this in the name of Jesus. Amen.

CHAPTER TEN

Blocking your stress cycles

"To everything there is a season, and a time for every
matter or purpose under heaven." (Ecclesiastes 3:1)

All *"life"* is programmed in cycles. No matter the subject: weather, the solar cycle, history, the economy, our bodies, we see the unfailing work of cycles. Cycles even govern our emotions, thought patterns, our self-images, and imaginations. We may be unaware of them, but they are there! We just don't pause long enough to connect the dots. Cycles are a mystery, which can only be explained in spiritual terms.

CYCLES IN HISTORY

Every empire and nation has its history patterned in cycles. The history of Israel and the United States reveal an astonishing array of multiple cycles guiding their destinies. Enormous stress is inflicted upon the peoples when negative cycles strike. Great blessings are poured out upon them when the cycles are positive.

Israel's history is replete with the phenomenon of cycles. From the time of King Saul (1 Samuel 10) to the captivity of Israel into Babylon in Zedekiah's reign, 450 years later, there were roughly 17 periods of great blessing visited upon the nation. Each period of prosperity was followed by deep valleys of economic ruin and depression as the nation sank into cycles of sin and idolatry.

All "life" is programmed in cycles. No matter the subject: weather, the solar cycle, history, the economy, our bodies, we see the unfailing work of cycles. Cycles even govern our thoughts and emotional lives.

The remarkable fact of eight major historical disasters, all occurring on the same day—the 9th day of Av—is far more than just coincidence. These eight tragedies were spread out over a period of thirty-five centuries!

Today, the infamous 9th of Av is Israel's day of mourning. A notable disaster occurring on that day was the destruction of the Temple in Jerusalem by King Nebuchadnezzar in 587 BC, (Jeremiah 52:5). Centuries later, the Temple was again destroyed, this time by the Roman General Titus in 70 AD, also on the 9th of Av. Even a brief study of this mysterious cycle would cause the most indurate heart to take note and wonder. This phenomenon is well documented in Grant Jeffrey's book *Unveiling Mysteries of the Bible* (Toronto, Ontario: Frontier Research Publications, 2002, page 123).

Cycles evident in America's history have also reaped both great stress and great blessings upon its people.

In the sequence of American presidents, the *"zero year factor"* provides an eerie look at the inner workings of cycles. Seven Presidents died in office when elected in a zero year. Perry Stone in his book, *Plucking the Eagles Wings* (Cleveland, Tennessee: Voice of Evangelism, page 118), lists twenty remarkable details, which link the assassination of Abraham Lincoln in 1865 (elected in a zero year) to the death of President Kennedy in 1960. Among those listed are: both Presidents had Vice Presidents named Johnson. The names of both Presidents had seven letters; Lincoln's secretary was Kennedy; Kennedy's secretary was named Lincoln; John Wilkes Booth (Lincoln's assassin) was born in 1839, Lee Harvey Oswald (Kennedy's assassin) was born in 1939, one hundred years apart! And so on…!

President Reagan was inaugurated in a zero year and was shot but not fatally. Since the power of these negative cycles resides in the spiritual realm, prayer can play a role in breaking or weakening the cycle. Interestingly, President Reagan was surrounded by strong prayer warriors throughout his tenure in the White House.

The evidence of Scripture clearly indicates that cycles operate by law. Ecclesiastes 1:9 alludes to its operating phenomena: *"The thing that has been—it is what will be again, and that which has been done is that which will be done again; and there is nothing new under the sun."* The Apostle Paul knew of the power of cycles and defines how they operate in our lives: *"In posing as judge and passing sentence on another, you condemn yourself; because you who judge are habitually practicing the very same things"* (Romans 2:1). *"For whatever a man sows, that and that only is what he will reap"* (Galatians 6:7).

HOW CYCLES WORK IN US

Cycles are triggered from our hidden negative responses to circumstances. Buried toxic emotions and beliefs rise to the surface of our minds on cue, and explode. They often leave us crying out in wonder: *"Here we go again!"*

We may be familiar with our responses, but not their cause. We are left with a choice: push them down or let what is in us fly!

When cycles strike, enormous stress may be placed upon the immune system, and other functions of the body. If we fail to pause and examine our emotions and thoughts at such times, we may miss an opportunity for healing. The cycle may continue on in its path, and may even grow over the years in intensity and frequency. Circumstances may differ, but their telltale emotional and mental signs are always the same.

Some cycles travel through families along generational lines. They follow curses down through three, or even four generations. When the circumstances are ripe, the cycle erupts, causing devastation upon the families, without them knowing why. Lamentations 5:7 illustrates this flowing down of cycles through family generations: *"Our fathers sinned and are no more, and we have borne their iniquities."*

Cycles tend to work against our godly desires, causing us to act out of character. Paul alluded to this feature of cycles in his own life, when he said: *"For I do not understand my own actions (I am baffled, bewildered). I do not practice or accomplish what I wish, but I do the very thing that I loathe (which my moral instinct condemns)"* (Romans 7:15-17). Compelling hidden forces made him act contrary to the will of the Spirit of God in him.

The Message Bible says it clearly this way:

> *"Something has gone wrong deep within me and gets the better of me every time. It happens so regularly that it's **predictable**. The moment I decide to do good, sin is there to trip me up. I truly delight in God's commands, but it's pretty obvious that not all of me join in that delight. Parts of me covertly rebel, and just when I least expect it, they take charge."* (Romans 7:15-17, MSG; Emphasis added).

A personal cycle

One cycle I was able to SEPARATE out, although hilarious as I see it now, was anything but at the time. It gave me a new appreciation of their power and persistence. I tracked this cycle back to my schooldays. Without warning, it violently crossed my life path. I had no control over when, or how, it would happen. It was as though some mischievous conductor was subtly orchestrating my world, my flesh, and the devil to induce fear and terror.

The earliest recollection of this cycle was at Grammar School in England. Each day, an irascible, yelling math teacher would seat herself on an empty desk in front of me, eagle-eyeing the class and my work from her high perch. Her piercing screams could be heard all over the school, but no one said anything.

Her daily assaults upon the class were mostly verbal, but at times, she wielded knuckles, rulers and any other implement she could find with great effectiveness. So great was the ordeal of that hour each day that my body developed deep, responsive memories to that class. In later life, any embarrassing situation would drop me back into that same room. I would manifest the same ugly dread and stress symptoms as those early school days.

A fireball of terror loosed itself from those years, which rolled across my life periodically and I had no idea how to stop it!

The next time the cycle appeared in force was at RAF boot camp, in south England. As a raw recruit, I was marched off the parade ground for what they thought was a smile on my straight face! In the middle of a windowless guardroom three starched corporals eyed me in silence, then, on cue, launched into a synchronized assault of ear-splitting percussions in my ears. My induction into their world of terror might have worked had I not already built steel walls around me, behind which I whispered: *"You can't hurt me. I've been here before!"* I knew how to push down the fear. I had built strong defensive walls.

Although this ball crossed my path several more times in later years, those protective walls let me get on with life. For a number of years the cycle never bothered me. That is, until I became a pastor! Four ladies decided they'd had enough of their rookie preacher. Without warning, they filed into my office after a service and let loose a fifteen-minute barrage of high verbal assaults, which were heard all over the church. I sat in silence, half amused by their ranting, safely hidden behind my protective shell.

What caused this cycle? Why did it carry such power? What started it? What gave it the energy? Only after entering the Elijah House training for inner healing, were my questions answered.

As I began to study this cycle, I realized that my trust in authority figures had been broken. I had developed a fear of them. Clearly, I had passed angry judgments against my schoolteacher and also had made a child's vow: *"No authority will ever get me into that position again."* A vicious cycle had been set in motion. It guaranteed that the same anger and bitterness would surface with its every appearance. That happened—except I had long since learned to cope by pushing down my feelings behind the bulwarks of my defense system.

In God's eyes my thinking was toxic: *"foolishness is bound up in the heart of a child, but the rod of discipline will drive it far from him"* (Proverbs 22:15).

Fifty years after it was birthed, this cycle finally lost its latent power. I had simply SEPARATED away all my feelings and thoughts from the memory and asked FORGIVENESS for judging my teacher.

THE ROOT SYSTEM OF CYCLES

At the core of every negative cycle is a strong belief system: a deeply embedded hurt, associated with angry judgments, and the expectation that it will happen again. They form the roots of the belief system which keep the cycle alive. But detecting these personal beliefs requires much prayer and help! This is why cycles are best seen in crises.

Bad news from the doctor, a financial reversal, the smell of smoke, a knife, some disappointment, an embarrassment, a single thought, a casual remark, a dream, a demand to speak before a group, any one of a 1001 shocks may disrupt our lives. All it would take for a cycle to trigger would be for some buried firecrackers of bitterness to go off in the subconscious mind. If there are hard judgments hiding below, powered by negative expectations, the flesh will immediately respond in a familiar outburst.

The most fertile years for the birthing of cycles are in childhood. They are initiated out of harsh, angry judgments made against another, upon oneself or even upon God.

The most fertile years for the birthing of cycles are in childhood. They are initiated out of harsh, angry judgments made against others, mostly on parents or upon oneself, or even upon God. This kind of bitter thinking lodges in our souls as open wounds. The Sandford's' popularized the term *"bitter-root judgments"* for our tendency to react to a hurt. They keep us insecure, with their cyclical patterns bearing down on us in waves.

If the original hurt remains unresolved, these underlying beliefs tend to strengthen as we get older. More lies, vows, and expectations are added to the core image of our bitterness. All it takes for the cycle to strike again is the right trigger!

The flesh, inspired by the devil, conspires to bring as much destruction as possible to his unwary victims. He may wait years before launching another assault on a victim. If a cycle can be activated in us, without exposing the hurtful memory and bitter root judgments below, the flesh can perpetuate its rotating annoyance *ad nauseam*. The flesh and the devil remain in control! They are able to keep their victims in bondage and block out Christ's wisdom and understanding. *"For My people are stupid; they do not know and understand Me. They are thickheaded children, and they have no understanding"* (Jeremiah 4:22).

All negatively charged cycles operate out of fear, and fall into the two main groups—**Shame** cycles and **Pride** cycles. As we saw in Chapter eight, our images hide in the subconscious mind and are perpetuated by unresolved hurts and bitter feelings. They form cyclical patterns in an individual's life, rolling forward on concealed negative expectations.

1. SHAME CYCLES

Shame cycles are always fear based. I lived the greater part of my life without recognizing that certain thoughts have the capability to trigger painful emotional cycles along my pathway. I had never bothered to isolate these cycles, and I was even less aware of their draining effects on me.

EXPECTATIONS ARE THE DRIVERS OF CYCLES

Fear-filled expectations drive our shame cycles. When we *expect* something to happen in a wrong way, it usually does. *"For the thing which I greatly fear comes upon me, and that of which I am afraid befalls me"* (Job 3:25).

Expectations are the mantras we carry around with us in ignorance of their power to disrupt our lives. Take a look at the list below and see if you recognize some of these very familiar statements. The more we repeat these mantras, the more they empower and perpetuate our cycles, keeping alive buried, angry judgments:

- *"I always panic in front of people"*
- *"I always feel like a failure next to him"*
- *"If I don't quit now, I will surely be embarrassed"*
- *"If I don't open my mouth—they won't see how dumb I am"*
- *"When things go wrong, I always get the blame"*
- *"I always feel ashamed and guilty in front of others"*

Here are a few examples from our casebook which demonstrate the power of shame-based expectations:

1. Cycles of the easily embarrassed

Fear of being embarrassed before others is a common expectation, especially in younger people. *Shame images* rise to pull us away to save face. Most learn to overcome this kind of invalidation of self as they grow older by pushing through the pain. But for others, the *expectation* of being embarrassed doesn't diminish in strength over the years, but rather gets stronger. They lurk in the back of the mind, ready to strike; all they need is an opportunity given by circumstances and another cycle is triggered.

Being embarrassed was like a bug in me that stung a thousand and one times in my earlier years. This inner fear of being *"put on the spot"* developed a cycle, which caused periodic excruciating waves of torment. Even in my twenties, I couldn't walk into a restaurant with more than two people already seated. If there was a line-up, I would walk around the block, a quarter of a mile, so as not to confront watching eyes!

This nest of hornets in my subconscious kept me always on guard! It reduced my life to narrow, highly predictable paths. Even in later years, this fear-filled expectation hovered menacingly in the background of my mind. I would go to great lengths to ensure the bug remained caged. But many times, I fell into the shame trap and had to suffer through the indignities of panicky symptoms I knew so well.

2. Cycles of a slow-poke!

Those unable to process thoughts fast enough to articulate them often feel ashamed and even guilty. In school, their slowness makes them a target for jokes. If the child responds in anger, bitterness may root in his heart. A cycle is then birthed, which may repeat all the emotional and mental patterns of early childhood many times through his life. Quick-witted Type "A's" love to provoke, interrupting slower people frequently, even finishing their tasks and sentences for them. But their unsolicited help is often seen as unloving, leaving behind churning anger, which accumulates as stress through the years.

Alice complained that her mom *"always finished her sentences for her!"* Those moments established a painful cycle in her life, which left her acutely embarrassed and ashamed. *"I was the slow-poke of the family!"* As a child she had judged her mom for making her life so hard, because she was so slow. It left deep scars. Later in life, the hurts still came, always for the same thing. Whenever she was with others she expected it would happen and it did. This had gone on all her life. *"When people interrupted me, it always felt like a put-down. I felt insecure and insignificant, as though I wasn't contributing anything. It made me withdraw into my little imaginary room of self-pity. I felt safe there!"*

When we went back through Alice's life, we found the bitter judgments that had established this painful cycle. It had run amok in her workplace, friendships and even into her marriage with her husband, and children. She tried to compensate for her slowness by trying to please, but this always seemed to leave her drained and worn out. As she grew older, the exhaustion stage of stress became so severe she sought help in counseling.

> When the bitter and angry roots of her judgments against her mom were brought to light, she asked for FORGIVE-NESS and repented of them before God. In a vision, she saw Jesus coming toward her imaginary safe room. She asked Him to smash it! Jesus pointed His finger at the room built out of lies. It glowed red, then exploded! No debris was left on her life path! The cycle that had been responsible for so much pain and isolation was finally gone! She was free from a pain she had carried since childhood.

3. Cycles of the suspicious

Suspicion is a prevalent, nervous spirit of our age, even in the Church. The flesh loves to compare and jump to conclusions—which are usually negative. We enjoy adding 2 + 2 to come up with 5. We analyze, draw conclusions about people and situations in our attempt to bolster our *Pride image*. We need an opinion to support our flagging *self.* Being suspicious is a loathsome mind-habit that God would rather have us do without. It is extremely stressful.

> **Suspicion is a prevalent, nervous spirit of our age, even in the Church. The flesh loves to compare and jump to conclusions—which are usually negative.**

Suspicion is a fruit of unresolved bitter judgments in the heart.

It is a form of worry. There is a wound of shame and rejection deep in the soul. It leaves victims constantly unsure whether others accept or love them. They live in dread of being cast aside again. Suspicion is a torment that ultimately stresses the immune system.

Madge couldn't stop jumping to conclusions and coming up with worst case scenarios. Each time circumstances triggered a fresh cycle, it threw her into spells of shame and guilt: *"What is wrong with me? Why do I keep doing this?"*

She had been trying to get hold of her friend, Cindy by phone. She had left a message on her answering machine. But her friend didn't return her call in the hour she expected. This delay triggered a familiar cycle of suspicion. *"I waited patiently, one hour then two, then two days and still no call. I tried to resist all temptation to question my friend's motives. Then I started to get emotional. I became impatient and frustrated. Negative thoughts swirled in my mind: 'She must be upset with me. I must have done something wrong.'"* Anger and bitter judgments were hurled at her friend. *"I don't need her as a friend. She's mean. I will never allow myself to get close to her again."* Then she was angry with herself for the way she was thinking: *"Why was this happening again?"* she wondered?

Suddenly, Cindy called: *"I have been in the hospital,"* she explained.

Madge felt ashamed and guilty at her immature, suspicious response. Once again, she had fallen into the familiar mind trap. As she SEPARATED out her bitter criticisms of her mom's impatient and suspicious nature toward her as a child, she realized she had been doing the exact same thing.

This highly stressful cycle came under new management of the Holy Spirit. She made up her mind before God not to fall into the same temptation again. The cycle lost its power as a stressor. FORGIVENESS brought her into Christ's peace and from that time on was aware of the trap. It made it easier to wait. She began to *listen* to what the Holy Spirit was telling her about such delays.

Supposing like this is an extremely common indulgence of the flesh, and it is hard to break. When we humbly bring these mindsets before the Lord, we see them for what they are—sin!

In this case, Madge's imagination regurgitated shame-based expectations she practiced as a child. Cindy's delayed phone call triggered the suspicion that once again she was being humiliated and rejected. It proved to be a cycle that needled and drained her. It had been a nuisance stressor all her life, as S.I.S—Self-Inflicted Stress.

God is looking for saints who will empty themselves of these troublemakers. It is time we allow the Holy Spirit to destroy these shameful foxes in the garden of our mind: *"Teach me Your way, O Lord, and lead me in a plain {and} even path because of my enemies [those who lie in wait for me.... Wait {and} hope for {and} expect the Lord"* (Psalms 27:11, 14).

2. PRIDE CYCLES

Pride cycles are much harder to detect than Shame cycles. Some individuals, even in the face of strong evidence, will vehemently deny their existence. Pride cycles form out of a deep psychological need to look good before others. A person abandoned in childhood will culti- vate prideful thoughts to overcome their handicap in an attempt to diminish their inner pain. They learn to walk through life with a *Pride image*, which manifests in periodic emotional upheavals in their lives.

Abused children, sensing rejection from their parents, will try to win their acceptance and love by *working* for it. They develop a prideful spirit out of their rejection and crushed identity. They may manipulate, exaggerate, and even lie in order to receive approval.

An entire life may be caught in this uncomfortable mindset of trying to please others to justify themselves and lift themselves up before others. Instead of seeking freedom from the pain of their childhood rejection, they build defensive walls around their hurts, and adopt aggressive attitudes to succeed.

Pleasing others is a natural expression of growing up. But if the habit persists into adult life, the need to impress others quickly turns into painful stressors; a vicious cycle is then birthed.

Geoff was asked to be "maintenance man" for a large church. He enjoyed the attention of his new boss for the first few weeks on the job. But a hidden prideful mindset again began to boil in him. Geoff had to be *seen, heard, accepted and praised.* This was the driving need and purpose of his life. A chronic fear of failing had trapped him into box thinking and passivity. *He couldn't afford to be rejected again.* These powerful expectations drove him to control every life situation— to be the boss, creating a cycle that delivered periodic knock-out punches every two or three years in his life.

His cycle had birthed in his childhood. Abandoned and brutally hurt by his dad, he grew up with deep hurts and rage. At times he felt good about himself, at other times crushed. His discordant thinking rolled him from periods of high self-exaltation down to lows of self-rejection, self-pity, depression, and near suicide.

To overcome his sense of worthlessness, he sought *titles* to go along with each job. It was the same in this new position. To impress his boss, he exaggerated the smallest success. Soon his boss began to distance himself; Geoff's frustrations began to mount. Isolated and feeling unwanted, Geoff finally quit. His cycle had struck again, on time, after two years.

When we tracked back Geoff's life cycles to childhood, we found the expectation that propelled his cycles, and the bitter hatred for his dad. Only then did he begin to see the roots of sin that sparked periodic destructions in his life.

People pleasers like Geoff find it hard to be real. They live their lives in an illusion through pride.

People pleasers like Geoff find it hard to be themselves. They live their lives acting out pride-filled illusions. Their expectation that *"I must be boss,"* becomes a shield to protect them from being hurt again, but this dooms them to a life defined by horrendously painful cycles. This makes lasting relationships difficult. A little child is still hurting in them, which becomes more visible as they get older!

The need to perform and to be perfect is a coping mechanism for an inner lack of love never realized as a child. A novice pastor will sometimes "fish" for compliments after each Sunday sermon. His focus is upon pleasing his people, not the Lord. When none are forthcoming, he deflates, worrying that others see him as a failure.

These childlike internal conversational responses are to be put away. God looks upon them as sin!

Author James Dobson blames parents for contributing to these unnatural expectations. Parents want super-kids. Their grades, their sports skills are worked over for high goals. The child sees that what he does is never good enough. He's caught in a cyclical trap of performing to please for love. Enormous pressure is placed upon him *'to look good,'* which then becomes a habit of life.

Striving to please our parents may be so strong that the victim continues the habit long after they have died!

JESUS TAUGHT ABOUT CYLES

Jesus pointed to the work of cycles in the Sermon on the Mount: *"For just as you judge {and} criticize {and} condemn others, you will be judged {and} criticized..."* (Matthew 7: 2) implies a living cycle and a warning for us. A critical remark tinged with anger acts like a bouncing ball. It returns in a 360-degree cycle—and in kind. Few Christians have this revelation. Judging others violates a law of

God—this one! By and large the warning is ignored. Jesus tells us that our conversation must be cleansed of every judgment and critical thought, if we are to know His peace.

When we see the light of this truth, the destructive power of critical words comes into view. We immediately resolve to guard our hearts and minds and to speak only words that lift others in Christ's love.

This Law was restated by the Apostle Paul: *"Do not be deceived and deluded and misled...for whatever a man sows, that and that only is what he will reap"* (Galatians 6:7). His graphic farming illustration tells us that our thinking operates in cycles. We have the capacity to not only choose the kinds of seeds we sow, but also to measure the harvest that will inevitably return to us! We must sensitize ourselves to the appetites and wills of the flesh, which is at *"war against the law of my mind (my reason), making me a prisoner to the law of sin* (and death) *that dwells in my bodily organs"* (Romans 7:23). Then, we are able to *see* the consequences of our actions, and cancel out the sowing from the reaping!

As believers, we are now living the Life of the Spirit, *"if the Holy Spirit of God (really) dwells within you (directs and controls you)"* (Romans 8: 9). We are being directed by new Laws written upon our hearts by the Holy Spirit.

This Law is different from the binding Law of the flesh, in that it gives Liberty and Life for every moment we choose to dwell upon the Lord Jesus Christ. By this divinely inspired Law, we are set free from the curse of negative cycles. *"For the Law of the Spirit of life which is in Christ Jesus, has freed me from the law of sin and death"* (Romans 8:2).

Delighting in the Law of God *"in my inmost self with my new nature* (Romans 7:22) turns us into godly merchants, dispensers of Christ's treasures and blessings. We are led of the Spirit to sow good *thought seeds* into the hearts and minds of others, causing measures of goodness to fall upon them and to initiate in them cycles that bless rather than curse. *"He who sows to the Spirit, will from the Spirit reap eternal life"* (Galatians 6:8).

When we come to look on our cycles objectively, we cannot

help but stand in amazement at the hidden forces of the fallen world, trying to control our destiny. We need to be free of them. Their firepower is the cause of much loss of energy and stress. As you begin the SEPARATION of your cycles, confess them before God and destroy their works on the Cross.

If we fail to separate the components of our cycles—our negative emotions, thoughts, images and imaginations—they will remain hidden and will continue to strike and inflict pain. By bringing them to the Cross in FORGIVENESS, they yield their power and Christ's peace is released.

ACTION PLAN FOR RECOVERY

I Principles

1. Negative cycles are triggered by our fleshly emotional and mental responses to circumstances. They operate under the law of sin and death.

2. These negative cycles are always birthed out of strong bitter judgments made against others—usually against our parents. If there is no FORGIVENESS, the cycles tend to intensify and become more frequent over time. A common exclamation accompanying cycles when they strike is: *"Here we go again!"*

3. Cycles absorb enormous amounts of energy, and impact the body through disruptions of the delicately balanced immune system.

4. To cancel our responses to these cycles, we must SEPA-RATE their negative elements, and bring them to the Cross in FORGIVENESS. The expectations of the cycles must be found, confessed and also be broken on the Cross. Locating hidden bitter judgments and the negative expectations in our cycles may require much prayer, but is an absolute require-ment for walking continually in Christ's peace.

II Questions

1. Scan over your childhood years and stop when you encounter a sudden traumatic experience. Note the emotions and thoughts around the trauma. Then see if there were similar 'events' that occurred as a crisis in your later years. Again note the emotions and thoughts. Look for repeating patterns; when did you last say: *"Oh no! Not again!"?*

2. Take a closer look at the pattern you have discovered. Then

look for the triggers to your cycles—that is, the strong expectations that propelled your cycles. In the earliest traumatic event you can remember in the sequence, what bitter judgments did you make against another?

3. Are you ready to FORGIVE the one who hurt you? Bring your pain, bitter judgments and expectations before Jesus in FORGIVENESS and repent. Stay in His presence until you sense there has been a complete exchange of your hurt for His peace.

III Prayer

Father, I have a new perspective on my life. So many times my life has been churned by destructive cycles. I want them stopped! I realize they are SELF-INFLICTED! Please FORGIVE me, Lord. Help me to find the bitter judgments I have made, and the negative expectations, which perpetuate these explosive cycles in my life. Help me to locate the times in my life when a cycle repeated itself and caused me much stress. I bring these cycles before You Lord. Help me to establish new cycles as I continue my walk with You. Thank You, Lord Jesus. You continually bless others and I want to do the same. I pray this in Jesus' name. Amen.

CHAPTER ELEVEN

Enjoying life in Christ's peace

*"I have told you these things, that My joy and delight may
be in you, and that your joy and gladness may be of full
measure and complete and overflowing."*
(John 15:11).

This study on stress was birthed out of one scripture: *"Peace I
leave with you, My [own] peace I now give and bequeath to
you"* (John 14:27). One question was always before me: *"Where
was it?"*

As the answers came, I realized that God had set me upon a
journey not only to come out of stress, but also to move deeper into
His peace and Holiness. Each stage of the journey led me into the
Word of God, and into the excitement of His revelations.

We have seen how *Stress* attacks every part of us. It starts
slowly, in secret, and then explodes in us. We have looked into its
symptoms, and how to manage their impact on the body. We also
looked into how we are to deal with the roots of stress to eliminate
their power. Two important keys were given. By faith filled application of these Keys a progressive walk into calmness and assurance
in Christ is established:

1. **The Key of SEPARATION**: God used the process of "SEPARATION" to bring order out of chaos—so must we. Separation from the world, flesh, and the devil and all that is negative is a requirement for every Christian. If we are to raise Christ's foundations of peace, joy, love, and humility in us, we must SEPARATE every ungodly emotion, thought pattern, image, imagination and cycle.

2. **The Key of FORGIVENESS**: This Key continues the process of Separation in us. By its constant use, we break the chains of bondage in us. The more we apply this Key, the more we sense freedom in Jesus. We feel more assured of our standing before God. This is true *sanctification,* and the result is a renewed mind accompanied with the peace of God.

Stress pressures will always be around us. We will be constantly subject to the *"presence of sin"* trying to control us until the day Jesus delivers us, either through death or the rapture of the Church. Our self nature cannot be destroyed entirely, but it can be immobilized on the Cross daily, by faith.

> **We will be subject to the *"presence of sin"* trying to control us until the day Jesus delivers us, either through death or the Rapture of the Church.**

ATTAINING CHRIST'S PEACE

Scripture tells us that in the last days God's people will know the fullness of Christ's peace, as we enter into the joy of the Lord (John 15:11).

In a world of increasing darkness, the saints of God will shine like the stars and lead multitudes to righteousness (Daniel 12:3). Christ Jesus will be the focus of all we feel, think, say, and do. We will sense the freedom and upward pull of the Holy Spirit in us. We are being raised in resurrection life from the dark realms of the world, the flesh and the devil.

Our world is changing rapidly—fear and stress levels are rising. But the message is clear: God is lifting His standard in the hearts of men (Isaiah 59:19). His glory is promised *upon* us and *His Presence* will be visible in us. This is the *Light* which will draw nations and kings to the brightness of His rising (Isaiah 60:1-3).

God is looking for those who are willing to live a SEPARATED life, walking continually in FORGIVENESS with the Separator—Jesus Christ. He is looking for a Bride, pure, radiant and passionately in love with the Groom—a body of people whose hearts are open and ready to hear their Master—the Lord Jesus Christ.

How do we enter into Christ's peace and stay in it? Is there a key we can take away with us and use every day?

The command *"Be still, and know (recognize and understand) that I am God"* (Psalms 46:10) is one of the least practiced life keys in the Church today. Sunday is often as hectic as every other day of the week. But this is what we need—a stillness that restores and heals. The word *still* is defined by The *New Strong's Complete Dictionary of Bible Words,*1996, published by Nelson, as *Peacefulness, silence, astonish, forsake, let alone* as well as *to mend, cure, heal, repair and to thoroughly make whole.*

This then, is our third Key:

Key #3: Stillness in the presence of God keeps us free from chaos.

Learning to be *still in the Spirit* is Jesus' most powerful antidote to stress, and is available to every Christian. Stillness not only protects our relationship with God, but is the means by which He nurtures our spirits. *"In returning [to Me] and resting [in Me] you shall be saved; in quietness and in [trusting] confidence shall be your strength"* (Isaiah 30:15b).

We, as believers, are to be walking vessels for Christ's peace, serenity, and stillness, bearing His Life in our fear-filled, hyper, sick world.

We cannot grow in Christ unless we accept this key and set aside time each day to get alone with God. This is why Jesus placed so much emphasis on letting us know who has this peace: *"Peace I leave with you: My (own) peace I now give and bequeath to you. Not as the world gives do I give to you"* (John 14:27).

Lake Pato in British Columbia is surrounded by snow-capped rugged peaks that dissolve in high clouds. By following a rocky path, the entire sweep of the turquoise lake is brought into view, filling every space like a soft, watercolor painting. Those snow-filled crevices and rocky abutments of the mountain faithfully reflect in the glassy stillness of the waters beneath. A single, purple streak separates land from sky.

This is how Jesus wants us to be—so still He can see the reflection of His character and nature in our personalities! We can only arrive at this goal through persistent practice of being still in His Presence.

Stress ruffles the waters of our souls each day. Waves of frustration, anger, bitterness, and disappointment wash away Christ's tranquil love, peace, and joy. Just as our parents told us "to be quiet," so Jesus is now telling us to do the same.

During many of my bouts with anxiety-panic attacks in the early hours of the morning, my only recourse was to cry up to the Lord for His mercy and intervention, At times, everything in me wanted to thrash around, scream, and jump over some imaginary cliff.

But God was always gracious. He would lead me to sit down in an easy chair, to breathe deliberately, steadily, and deeply. As my body quieted, the gentle pull of the Holy Spirit was always there, to draw me deeper into my Father's loving arms. Without my knowing it, the Lord was teaching me the art of being still in His presence. With practice I found I could rest in His presence without any difficulty. Several times I heard the still small voice within gently whisper in the early hours: *"All your anxiety has gone! It's time to go back to bed."* I would look at my watch and found

I had been with Him for over an hour, sometimes even two!

Quietness in the Spirit is not only a stress buster; it's also a flesh crusher!

The Psalmist shows us the purpose for this stillness: *"Surely I have calmed and quieted my soul......... like a weaned child is my soul within me (ceased from fretting)"* (Psalm 131:2). God has given us the responsibility to silence the worrying and fretting working in our flesh, in order that we may channel our energies into finding Him!

By extending our daily moments *of "resting"* in Christ each day, starting with one or two minutes, the mind will gradually submit to the new management. You will find, as I did that you will strive less. Tasks seem easier and there are fewer emotional upheavals over minor events. Your relationship with God will be strengthened.

Quietness in the Spirit is not only a stress buster; it's also a flesh crusher!

How do we know we have made contact with the living God in our quiet times?

When all the mind chatter ceases; when all condemnation, shame, fear, guilt, and pride, and every negative thought leaves our minds—we are in the Spirit. Our focus is solely upon Jesus. Only then do we realize that greater is He who is within us than he that is in the world (1John 4:4).

Self cannot be killed, but we are able to *reckon* this villain as dead by faith *"Even so consider yourselves also dead to sin and your relation to it broken, but alive to God"* (Romans 6:11). We command its submission to our new, redeemed will and it must obey. Then, we find we no longer respond in the way we once did to adverse circumstances; our flesh with all its negative emotions, desires and thinking, is considered *"nailed to the Cross"* (Romans 6:6).

Worry and uptightness, are sure signs our flesh has become active again! This is why learning the art of being still in Christ is a practice every Christian should learn. Jesus has given us the right to use this stillness as a shield against the devil at anytime. Satan cannot penetrate the boundaries of this shield: we are hidden in Christ. Stress is held in check—on the Cross!

Stillness in the Spirit is the greatest treasure a believer can possess. In cultivating this calmness, we gradually eliminate every wish to be someplace else. One desire remains: to be with Jesus at peace.

Jesus desires we live every day celebrating *"moments"* of time, not in five-year projections. This was the choice I consciously made and practiced to combat the armies of worry and anxiety. *"So do not worry or be anxious about tomorrow, for tomorrow will have worries and anxieties of its own. Sufficient for each day is its own trouble"* (Matthew 6:34). Each moment offers an opportunity to find this jewel of stillness and Christ's peace, which bring with it a sense of belonging and destiny.

1. SEE THE FUN SIDE OF THINGS—AND SMILE!

Everything starts with a choice. *"See, I have set before you this day life and good, and death and evil"* (Deuteronomy 30:15). Calmness and a sense of assurance in Jesus Christ enable us to relax enough to see the fun side of everything. We become like children ready to receive everything that God offers from His storehouse and finding it fun!

Few Christians ever think of the Father in Heaven smiling. But He does! His humor is gentle and honoring to Himself and us. You might see His smile in a rainbow, a snow-capped mountain range, or a sunset over a lake, even in a duck! His smile is there waiting for us to share in the moment.

Jesus and the Holy Spirit have this same humor. They all have funny bones; so should we! Our new birth in Christ bears the gene not only of peace and stillness but also of joy! (Romans 14:17).

Carol and I were able to observe the power of this kind of smiling in our dear friend Cecilia, stricken with cancer in the hospital. In the midst of her raking sickness, she chose life: her radiant smile and calmness were a powerful testimony of her love for Jesus Christ. Even the seemingly insignificant was to Cecilia pure joy, and fresh evidence of the goodness of God: a gentle, cooling breeze from the open window touching her face; a child running in the corridor; the Word of God read at her bedside; a freshly cut flower on her side table were all occasions for a smile. She had chosen to release the peace and joy of Christ that were within her.

Start by wearing a smile within—all day long, like Cecilia. Soon it will appear on the outside! Smiling within is a switch that turns on our sense of Christ in us, by faith. Suddenly, we feel calm! One smile, or one encouraging word, will trigger reciprocal responses in others. Smiles are contagious de-stressors: they spread like fire!

Mother Teresa once said: *"Smile at each other, smile at your wife, smile at your husband, smile at your children, and smile at each other— it doesn't matter who it is — that will help you grow in greater love for each other."*

Wear a smile within all day long and soon it will appear on the outside!

Find opportunities to smile and laugh at just about anything, and you'll find a praise wall goes up before you, blocking the fiery darts of worry and fear. You will be less likely to feel hurt and put down; mistakes won't bother you the same. In tense situations, use a smile as you would a stealth weapon to disarm the devil. When someone frustrates you or makes you feel embarrassed, practice the silent smile. Stay peaceful within. This will give you time to gather your thoughts, rather than negative emotions and thoughts gathering you! A silent smile is disarming: it stops any attempt of others to control you.

Shakespeare said in the *Taming of the Shrew*: *"Frame your mind to mirth and merriment, which bars a thousand harms, and lengthens life."*(Line 295*).* Solomon's words are also as fresh today as when they were first penned: *"A merry heart does good like medicine, but a broken spirit dries the bones"* (Proverbs 17:22, NKJV).

More than any other factor that helped de-stress my life was this helpful tip of learning to see the fun side of things. Enjoying the *now* moments of God set me free from striving and expecting. As I practiced wearing a smile within, a calm delight began to settle in me, which came out as encouragement to others.

The Lord gave a picture about this just as I was waking from a restful sleep. I saw myself sauntering along the centre of an empty boulevard, at night, banked on both sides by high rise buildings, shining their lights on me below. I was wrapped in coarse dull brown sackcloth and a floppy hat of the same material. Lost in wonder and smiling, I watched as small and large bubbles erupted from my mouth, floating upward in praise to God.

After I had related this to Carol, she reminded me of John 4:14, which speaks of the living water rising and spilling out, *bubbling up* from deep within. It was confirmation of the victory the Lord had worked in me.

Laugh from a grateful heart

Exuberant laughing is a gentle form of aerobic exercise.

Exuberant laughing is a gentle form of aerobic exercise. It strengthens the heart and tones the mind. Robert R. Provine in his book on *Laughter* (New York: Penguin Group, 2000, page 212), suggests lowering your threshold of laughter by adopting *"a laugh-ready attitude."* Just be willing and prepared to chuckle and laugh at any time. Expect to enjoy yourself and you will. It is a self-fulfilling prophecy.

There is no doubt that laughter helps raise serotonin levels and acts like medicine. According to Dr. Colbert, a good belly laugh lowers adrenaline by as much as 70%. Cortisol levels drop by 40%. T-cells and interferon increase. Stress, in its many forms—depression, grief, sadness, and anger—always gives way to smiling or laughing.

Habitually smiling and laughing people derive their joy from a grateful heart. The Apostle Paul recommends we cultivate an attitude of gratefulness in all things. We are to thank God even for the trials we go through. He entreats us to *"rejoice in the Lord always."* When we set out to practice the principles of thanksgiving and gratefulness, we model the positive mindset of Paul, *"and the God of peace (of untroubled, undisturbed well being) will be with you"* (Philippians 4:4, 9).

During one desperate moment in an anxiety-panic attack that suddenly erupted in the early hours of the morning, I thought my end had come and prepared myself to scribble out some final instructions for Carol. From somewhere deep within came the still small voice of God that simply said: *"Give Me thanks."* It seemed an impossible transition to make, even an unreasonable request. Even to give thanks meant I had somehow to think clearly enough to grasp the thought and summon enough energy to speak it out! But I did.

Within seconds a wave of Christ's peace came over me, sufficient to let me get back to bed and sleep. That morning, in a half sleep, I entered into a vivid experience in the Presence of God during which He sovereignly delivered me from the tensions beneath my chest. God delights in our obedience. He cherishes our willingness to remember Him even in our worst moments by giving thanks.

A laughing, smiling, grateful saint is a great asset to the Body of Christ. He has not only learnt to be still and thankful before God, he has set himself as a *'standard'* before others. What he practices in his heart eventually comes out of his mouth. *"For out of the fullness (the overflow, the superabundance) of the heart, the mouth speaks."* (Matthew 12:34b).

2. CULTIVATE A HOLY SPIRIT-DIRECTED MOUTH

Every Christian needs to know the power contained in the words that fall from his mouth.

In the Creation story (Genesis 1:3-30), words spoken from the lips of God had power enough to SEPARATE away all that was not good, and power enough to redraw the map of earth with all that was good. That is how we should use our mouth: speaking words from our mouth that brings life to others.

A controlled mouth under the direction of the Holy Spirit indicates an inner stillness, a resting of the soul in Christ. Every word is measured against the standards of Jesus: *What would Jesus say in this situation? What feelings would He express? Would He hurt another deliberately with His words?* As we learn to align our speech to the words of Jesus a great calmness and freedom comes upon us. We no longer need to strive or worry. Proverbs 21:23 says it this way: *"He who guards his mouth and his tongue keeps himself from troubles."* This is the way stress is de-fanged!

Learn to speak only positive words

A heart that has learned to be still in Jesus will constantly affirm itself in Christ's Words.

Speak positively about yourself—say only what God says about you. No longer speak out what Satan says about you. Don't list your faults when things go wrong. We have a new positive Way in Christ. Even in problems, we must learn to speak into them with faith words.

David spoke victory before he could see it (1 Samuel 17:45-49): *"The Lord will deliver you* [his problem was Goliath] *into my hand."* This is using our mouth in the way God intended—in faith.

Positive faith affirmations help us to develop strong new mindsets. For every one time the devil whispers: *"God does not love you,"* speak back ten affirmations that He does.

Building a list of positive affirmations is like carrying manna in a basket. Eat the promises of the Word at every opportunity—even a hundred times a day, if necessary. This will beat off the enemy. Make cue cards out of them. Whenever you feel down or stressed out, use one. They will remind you of who you are and of your new life in Jesus Christ.

Here are some you can use:

- *"God approves of me"*
- *"God loves me for who I am"*
- *"God is pleased with me"*
- *"God sees me as His child"*
- *"God has a good plan for me"*
- *"I am the head not the tail"*
- *"I am a blessing to every one I meet"*
- *"I am an overcomer"*
- *"I am enjoying every moment with Jesus"*
- *"I am loved by God, even when I make a mistake"*
- *"I am who God says I am"*

A Christian whose mouth is controlled by the Holy Spirit scatters good seed. *"The lips of the wise disperse knowledge sifting it as chaff from the grain"* (Proverbs 15:7). Ask the Holy Spirit to bridle your mouth each morning. Make it your mission to help others walk out of their S.I.S.

One of the greatest benefits of learning to walk in the liberty of Christ, free from self-inflicted stress is that the blessings of the Lord began to overtake us.

This is a promise God gives to those of His children who will listen diligently to the voice of the Lord and who will *"watch to do all His commandments."* Then *"the Lord your God will set you high above the nations of the earth. And all these blessings shall come upon you and overtake you"* (Deuteronomy 28:1-2).

Abundance is the nature of God's desire for His people:

"Beloved, I pray that you may prosper in every way and (that your body) may keep well, even as (I know) your soul keeps well and prospers" (3 John 2). As our minds stay with Jesus, God moves the storehouse of abundance from behind to the front of us, so that we can see it! *"The thief comes only in order to steal and kill and destroy. I came that they might have and enjoy life, and have it in abundance (to the full, till it overflows)"* (John 10:10).

If have read this work to this point, you should congratulate yourself. You have begun a good work and God will finish it! (Philippians 1:6). You have knowledge enough to de-stress yourself! Now it is up to you, to ask for the wisdom to apply it in your daily life.

It is our prayer that you will practice the ways suggested in this book to de-stress yourself. James 1:22 says we are to be *"doers of the word, and not hearers only, deceiving yourselves"* (NKJV). Truth will deceive if it remains mere knowledge. Christ's Truth, once received by us, makes us immediately accountable to Him. We must do something with it. Applying these three Keys will enable you to cross new thresholds of peace in Jesus Christ:

- **The Key of Separation**: separates us from all ungodly elements and is the first step to peace.

- **The Key of Forgiveness**: delivers us from bondage so that we may enter into Christ's peace.

- **The Key of Stillness:** brings us into Christ's Presence, which keeps us in His perfect peace.

I pray that you will use these Keys as constant reminders that, as a believer, you may walk in this world not only free from self-inflicted stress, but also in the holiness of the Lord Jesus Christ. As Paul said: *"I press on toward the goal to win the (supreme and heavenly) prize to which God in Christ Jesus is calling us upward"* (Philippians 3:14).

Now that the stress in your body is under control and you have freed yourself from the pains of shame and rejection, share your victory with your friends. You will be surprised at the number you find who suffer from varying degrees of Self-Inflicted-Stress. They will be the ones you will be able to help strengthen their walk in Jesus.

ACTION PLAN FOR RECOVERY

I Principles

1. Stillness is the key we use to enter into God's rest. Stillness in the Spirit of God quiets the spirit, soul, and body. In His stillness we reflect the character of the Lord Jesus Christ.

2. Learning to smile within is an important principle in learning how to stir up the gift that is within us.

II Questions

1. *"The command 'Be still and know that 1 am God'* (Psalms 46:10) *is one of the least practiced life keys in the Church today."*

Be honest. How much of your day do you give to God? Is it quality time? Are you being still in His Presence? Why not now make this a daily part of your life. Begin with 5 minutes each day, and then aim for a half hour, then one hour. If possible, make sure it is always at the same time; change the atmosphere with anointed music to help you become still.

2. *"Positive faith affirmations help us to develop strong new mindsets."*

Have you ever written out for yourself a list of positive godly affirmations, to develop a new image of yourself in Christ? Why not start now! Add one per day. Repeat them, dozens, even hundreds of time a day if you are going through a crisis and are not sure who you are. In time, the IMAGE OF CHRIST will be formed in you.

III Prayer

Father, I thank you for the treasure of Your peace You have deposited in me. I will treasure it. I will never knowingly allow the forces of the world, the flesh, and the devil to rob me of Your gift. I desire to be free of all stress. I will pursue Your peace and guard it diligently. I promise to give You more of my time. I desire more than anything to be still in You and to sense Your heart and Your love for me.

Help me to be one who always encourages with a smile, with a godly word for every occasion. Thank you for showing me the roots of stress and how to successfully de-fang it. Help me to share with others the Keys You have shown me in walking out of Self-Inflicted Stress. I pray this in the Name of Jesus Christ. Amen.

MAKING A DECISION FOR CHRIST

If you have never declared Jesus to be your Savior and the Lord of your life, we invite you now to make sure of your place with Jesus in His Kingdom.

God loves you and wants the best for you. He wants you to live every day in His peace and joy—stress free. Jesus died on the Cross for you. He conquered all sin. Now it is our turn. Everyone who comes to Him is given the opportunity to wipe all sin from his soul. If you ask Him into your heart, He will forgive you, wash you clean with His blood; write your name in the Lamb's Book of Life; and give you eternal life, with a home in Heaven. He will set you on a journey into health and strength, enabling you to do exploits for Him. The Holy Spirit will come and dwell in you, and lead you into full restoration by the resurrection power of Jesus Christ.

Father, I confess that I have allowed my heart and mind to be used in negative and often sinful ways. I now realize that my life has been shaped in sin. I believe, Father, that You raised Jesus from the dead, so that I may have resurrection life and live in Christ's peace, free from stress. Please forgive me for all of my sins. I receive You now, Jesus, as my Savior and Lord. Come and dwell in my heart. I receive the gift of Your righteousness and peace. My one desire now is to serve You and to bring honor to Your Name. Thank You for saving me and making me Your child.

Father, I ask for the gift of the Holy Spirit. Fill my heart with Your peace and love. I thank You for showing me how to live like You. Thank You Lord Jesus, Amen.

If you have prayed this prayer, you are born again, a part of the family of God. The Holy Spirit is now beginning a good work in you, sanctifying your heart and mind. *"Let"* Him have His way in you. Thank Him always for your new life in Him—stress free!

Bibliography

Books

Alcorn, Randy & Nancy. *Women Under Stress.* 1986 Multnomah, Portland Oregon

Brown, Barbara B. *Between Health and Illness.* 1985. Bantam Books. New York

Eliot, Robert M.D. *From Stress to Strength.* 1994. Bantam Books. New York

Hart, A. M.D. *Adrenaline and Stress,* 1995. W. Publishing Group, Division of Thomas Nelson Inc.

Hepden, Steve. *Explaining Rejection.* 1992. Sovereign World Limited. Kent, England

Kuyper, Vicki. *If I really wanted to Beat Stress.* River Oak Publishing, Tulsa, Oklahoma

Meyers, Joyce. *Managing Your Emotions.* 1997 Harrison House, Tulsa, Oklahoma

Meyers, Joyce. *Help Me I'm Stressed.* 1998. Harrison House, Tulsa, Oklahoma

Maccaro, Janet. Ph.D. *Breaking the Grip of Dangerous Emotions.* 2001. Siloam Press, Lake Mary, Florida

Mullen, Grant. M.D. *Why do I feel so down, When my faith should lift me up?* 1999. Sovereign World Ltd. Kent England

Roger, John & Peter McWilliams. You *Can't Afford the Luxury of a Negative Thought.* 1991 Prelude Press, Los Angeles, California

LaHaye, Tim Dr. *How to Win Over Depression.* 1988. Bantam Books, Toronto, Canada

Sandford, Paula. *Healing Women's Emotions.* 1992. Victory House. Tulsa, Oklahoma

Sandford, John & Paula. *Healing the Wounded Spirit,* 1985, Victory House. Tulsa, Oklahoma

Printed in the United Kingdom
by Lightning Source UK Ltd.
105133UKS00001B/334-357